BUSES

YEARBOOK 2016

Edited by STEWART J. BROWN

PUBLISHING

KEY

BUSES
YEARBOOK 2016

FRONT COVER: **A new Routemaster in the Go-Ahead fleet, LT275 (LT 1275), heads south across Westminster Bridge in May 2015.** PETER ROWLANDS.

BACK COVER (UPPER): **Photographed in 1965 on Edinburgh's High Street is one of Edinburgh Corporation's 100 Weymann-bodied Leyland Tiger Cubs bought in 1959-61 to replace a fleet of elderly single-deckers. This Tiger Cub was sold, with 47 others, to the Ulster Transport Authority in 1966 when removal of low bridges and road-lowering rendered them surplus to Edinburgh's requirements.** GAVIN BOOTH

BACK COVER (LOWER): **The so-called 'Barbie 2' livery for older vehicles, on a First Devon & Cornwall Leyland Olympian at Sennen Cove in 2007. This Alexander-bodied bus was new to Grampian in 1985.** STEVE RICE

PREVIOUS PAGE: **In Scarlet livery, a Reading gas-powered Scania K270 with Enviro300 SG bodywork.** PETER ROWLANDS

Published by Key Publishing Ltd.
www.keypublishing.com

First Published July 2015

ISBN: 978-1-910415-32-0

Printed in England by Berforts Information Press Ltd 23-25 Gunnels Wood Park, Stevenage, Hertfordshire, SG1 2BH

www.busesmag.com

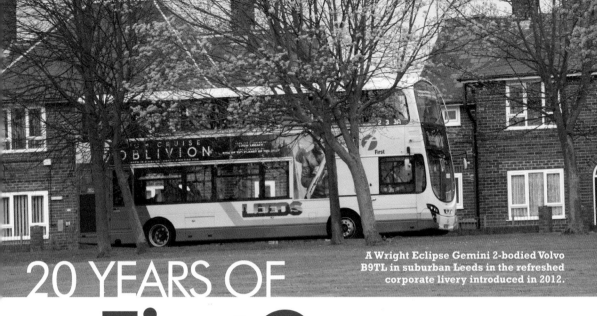

A Wright Eclipse Gemini 2-bodied Volvo
B9TL in suburban Leeds in the refreshed
corporate livery introduced in 2012.

20 YEARS OF

FirstGroup

Buses editor **ALAN MILLAR** looks back at the changing fortunes of the operator that for around 15 years was the largest in the UK.

I t was the first — and at the time of writing remains the only — merger of two of the UK's City-listed bus groups.

There may well be more in the future as the industry matures and adapts to change, but for now the combination of Badgerline Group and GRT Bus Group to form what then was called FirstBus — completed on 16 June 1995 — was a unique event in the rapid restructure of a much reorganised bus industry.

Badgerline and GRT had emerged from the privatisation programmes of the 1980s and early 1990s and were part of a move by all the major players to list their businesses on the London Stock Exchange to raise the money they needed for future investment and expansion. Badgerline had been listed since November 1993 and GRT since May 1994.

The same process saw National Express Group listed in December 1992, Stagecoach in April 1993 and Go-Ahead Group in May 1994.

The Badgerline cartoon badger on the side of a Leyland Lynx in the Brewers fleet in South Wales.

One other City-listed group also became part of this process: T. Cowie, then a car dealership and vehicle leasing business that happened also to own the Grey-Green coach and bus company in London, had been listed since December 1964. It made serious acquisitions in the bus sector at home and abroad from 1994, changed its name to Arriva in 1997 and had exited the car and van markets by 2006; it was delisted in August 2010 after selling out to Deutsche Bahn, the state-owned German railway.

Badgerline was the longer established and bigger of the two component parts of FirstBus, providing around 4,000 of the initial fleet of 5,600 buses. It grew out of the break-up and privatisation of the National Bus Company and the management buy-out of Badgerline, the third NBC subsidiary to be sold, in September 1986.

3

to acquire other businesses, mainly also ex-NBC companies.

By the time Badgerline was floated on the stock exchange, its acquisitions included City Line and Wessex in Bristol, Western National in Cornwall and parts of Devon, Eastern National and Thamesway in Essex and parts of London, South Wales Transport and regional sister company Brewers, and Midland Red West in Worcestershire, Herefordshire and operating into Birmingham.

It went on to make two significant acquisitions in 1994: PMT (another product of NBC privatisation) in Staffordshire, Cheshire and part of Greater Manchester; and Rider Group, the employee-owned former West Yorkshire PTE undertaking that had expanded into York when it purchased parts of the ex-NBC West Yorkshire Road Car Company. It paid £23million for PMT and £38million for Rider. Badgerline also had a stake in the Great Western train company, then providing inter-city services out of London Paddington.

GRT stood for Grampian Regional Transport and was the management/employee team that acquired the former Aberdeen municipal undertaking from Grampian Regional Council in January 1989. It was only the fifth arms length British municipal bus company to be privatised and the first public sector Scottish operator to go to the private sector.

It was based in Weston-super-Mare and operated former Bristol Omnibus Company services around Bristol, Bath, Weston and Wells.

Being so quick off the starting blocks, the Badgerline team had sealed their deal a month before the distraction of deregulation and without the price being driven up by any competing bids. They secured £4.5million of assets — including around 400 buses — for just £2.3million. They also were well placed

Barbie livery on a Wright Pathfinder-bodied Dennis Lance SLF, a pioneering low-floor bus built for London in 1994 and cascaded to First Midlands West — minus its centre doors — by 2007.

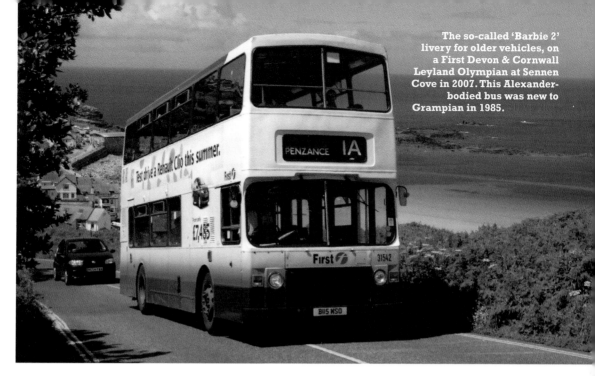

The so-called 'Barbie 2' livery for older vehicles, on a First Devon & Cornwall Leyland Olympian at Sennen Cove in 2007. This Alexander-bodied bus was new to Grampian in 1985.

There was a lot more knowledge of the value of privatised bus companies by then, obliging the GRT team to pay £5.5million for a business running around 225 vehicles.

The trigger for the GRT team to bid for their business was the government announcement in 1988 that the state-owned Scottish Bus Group would follow NBC in being broken up and sold. They feared that an energised Northern Scottish company could possibly acquire them or drive them out of business.

Instead, GRT was ready to bid when SBG was privatised and in 1990 acquired Midland Bluebird, the second subsidiary to be sold. By the time it floated on the stock exchange, it had moved into England to acquire two of the first arms length municipal companies to be sold on the open market, Northampton Transport and Leicester Citybus.

City listing provided the funds to buy two management/employee-owned ex-SBG companies, Lowland and SMT serving Edinburgh, the Lothians and Borders, and management-owned ex-NBC subsidiary Eastern Counties in Norfolk and Suffolk.

MERGER OR TAKEOVER?

The decision to create FirstBus had grown out of a meeting in Edinburgh between the two groups' chairmen, Badgerline's Trevor Smallwood and GRT's Moir Lockhead, where they concluded that they might progress better as one business.

First has occasionally supplemented its purchase of new vehicles with secondhand purchases. Among them were 50 Northern Counties Palatine-bodied Volvo Olympians that Stagecoach leased for seven years and First bought in 2003. This one, operating for First Scotland East in Stirling in 2009, was one of 33 originally with Cambus.

Both hailed from the north of England and had begun their bus industry careers in modest positions, Rotherham-born Smallwood in 1966 as a teenage traffic trainee with Yorkshire Traction, Lockhead — from a Co. Durham mining community — as a 15-year-old apprentice mechanic with United Auto six years earlier. Smallwood had been running what became the original Badgerline company since 1983, while Lockhead moved from engineering to general management in 1985 to head the Grampian business.

5

Articulated buses included 40 Volvo B10LAs with Wright Fusion bodies, 10 of which were new to First Glasgow in 2009. Like similar bendybuses in other First fleets, they ran usually with only the front doors in use.

Smallwood became chairman of FirstBus, Lockhead chief executive and deputy chairman. Like GRT, it was registered in Scotland and there were two head offices, GRT's in Aberdeen and Badgerline's at Badger House, a converted farmhouse outside Weston.

Subsequent events lend strength to the perception of who really was in charge. The clues lie in the country of registration and which of the pair had the key day-to-day role as chief executive. Smallwood retired in 1999, aged 52, devoting his time to charitable and other business interests.

Back in 1995, someone at Badgerline is alleged to have quipped that what was painted as a merger was 'really a takeover by GRT but Trevor doesn't know it yet'. When I had an opportunity to interview Lockhead in January 2009, as he celebrated the 20th anniversary of the GRT buyout, he dismissed that as other people's perceptions

'We never felt that. We all saw it as a merger of two companies that got on well, and from then on we really took off.'

Although smaller than Stagecoach at its formation, from the outset FirstBus was intent on becoming the biggest UK bus operator and embarked on a series of acquisitions, some of them eye-wateringly large, eventually operating over 9,000 buses here.

Before 1995 was out it acquired People's Provincial in Hampshire, one of only two NBC subsidiaries sold to their employees, and bought Stagecoach's 20% shareholding in Mainline, the former South Yorkshire PTE company.

Its biggest deals came in 1996 with the purchase of the 950-vehicle GM Buses North — half of the former Greater Manchester PTE operation — and the 1,250-vehicle SB Holdings in Greater Glasgow, which combined the former Strathclyde PTE bus operation with the ex-SBG Kelvin Central company. Stagecoach also had a 21.7% shareholding in SB, but as at Mainline had been ordered to sell it following a Monopolies & Mergers Commission judgment. First offered £47million for GMB North, £96million for SB.

While these deals hugely increased its presence in large city regions, First also consolidated its position in Hampshire by acquiring Transit Holdings' operation in Portsmouth and bought the Blue Bus municipal company in Great Yarmouth. Another piece of the

The London operation was a source of large numbers of double-deckers transferred mid-life to regional fleets. This TransBus President-bodied Volvo B7TL was working for First Glasgow in 2015.

Hampshire jigsaw followed in 1997 with the purchase of employee-owned Southampton Citybus.

Of more strategic importance, 1997 took First into London. Badgerline and GRT had missed out on the privatisation of the 10 London Buses subsidiaries in 1994, when Cowie, Go-Ahead and Stagecoach had acquired five of the six companies sold to outside buyers.

A £54million deal bought it management/employee-owned CentreWest, which since 1994 had acquired the ex-NBC Beeline business in Berkshire and had an interest in Croydon Tramlink. It also brought one of the most talented busmen of his generation — CentreWest managing director Peter Hendy — into the business, in which he rose rapidly to become deputy director of UK bus operations before leaving in 2000 to begin a stellar career at Transport for London, becoming its commissioner — in charge of the entire organisation — in 2006, earning a knighthood in 2013 and then becoming chairman of Network Rail in 2015.

The London business grew in 1998 with the purchase of one of the largest independents, Capital Citybus, which a management team led by Leon Daniels — who followed Hendy to a senior post at TfL in 2011 — had acquired from Hong Kong-based owners two-and-a-half years earlier. Daniels held senior group roles at First for more than 10 years.

First acquired full ownership of Mainline in 1998 — the year the group name changed to FirstGroup as it increased its involvement in railways — and its final major territorial expansion came in 1999 with the £10.6million acquisition of Cawlett Holdings' North Devon Red Bus and Southern National businesses in Dorset, Devon and Somerset, one of the few ex-NBC companies by then still owned by its former management. It bought the Chester municipal company in 2007.

While Stagecoach's expansion over this period brought several confrontations with the competition authorities, First had a nearly charmed existence by comparison. Except once when it escaped by the skin of its teeth.

The SB Holdings purchase came in the last year of John Major's Conservative government and gave First dominant coverage across central Scotland, from west of Glasgow to east of Edinburgh. The Monopolies & Mergers Commission thought this was excessive and persuaded the then trade minister that part of the combined business should be sold.

First had the option of selling all of SB or else a quarter of the Glasgow business and all of Midland Bluebird, which by then had absorbed part of SMT. It protested against the decision and persuaded the incoming Labour government that it could keep it all in return for undertakings on its future behaviour.

It was lucky all this happened then and not five years later, for the MMC's successor, the Competition Commission, gained powers in 2002 that removed politicians' final say in its decisions.

CREATING A BRAND

Bringing all these bus operations together was a challenge, for here was a large business made up of privatised NBC, SBG, municipal and PTE undertakings and in Capital Citybus one large independent. Each had its own operating culture, and the management styles at Badgerline and GRT were also quite different, with GRT's being more of a top-down approach while Badgerline exercised a lighter touch.

Consider also two of the things more visible to the outside world: liveries and vehicle purchases. Badgerline had no corporate livery, just a logo, a benign black and white cartoon badger displayed next to the rear

A 2011 view of an Alexander Dennis Enviro200 of First London on Waterloo Bridge.

wheels of its buses. Otherwise they wore bright colour combinations — for example, green and yellow at Eastern National, red at yellow at PMT — in different styles.

GRT had a corporate livery style of cream with local colour (green for Grampian, blue for Midland Bluebird, red for Leicester, Northampton or Eastern Counties) and a fleetname in a typeface that incorporated a thistle as the dot above the letter 'i'. This preserved a local identity while also developing a single brand.

First took time to develop its own identity, though the badger logos were soon peeled off. 'Welcome to FirstBus' stickers — in a new corporate style with a stylised letter *f* and without either a dot or thistle in the 'i' — appeared quickly in side windows, the Welsh language version of 'Croeso i BwsCyntaf' running the risk of being mispronounced as an Anglo-Saxon obscenity.

The Greater Manchester fleet was rebranded from orange, black, grey and white to allover orange, Greater Glasgow's from orange and black, red and cream or green and yellow to allover red, while Provincial — devoid of its erstwhile People — ditched its historic green for cream and red.

Fleetnames were initially those of the subsidiary companies, altered to the new corporate typeface, still in one of the colours of the local livery, but that changed from the end of 1997 with the beginnings of uniformity.

First became the main fleetname in large letters, with the local name appearing smaller above the nearside front wheel and below the driver's side window. Some local names became more geographical than historic, for example Midland Bluebird and SMT changing to Edinburgh even on buses that never ventured near the Scottish capital. Eventually, the local names were ditched completely.

Local colours vanished in two stages. The first stage introduced a standard corporate livery on new vehicles only. This was off-white with dark blue and magenta bands and a willow leaf pattern towards the back, nicknamed by someone as 'Barbie' because of the resemblance to the packaging of Mattel's globally successful doll.

This accompanied a new standard interior with similar pastel shades — including pale green handrails — apparently intended to make bus travel more appealing to women.

On normal replacement cycles, it would have taken at least until 2012 for the entire fleet to be in corporate livery, leaving the users of locally liveried buses with a clear impression that they were receiving a substandard product. So early 2001 ushered in the application of a simplified corporate livery for pre-1997 vehicles, the so-called 'Barbie 2' style with fade-out magenta vinyls and not so much as a willow twig, never mind a leaf.

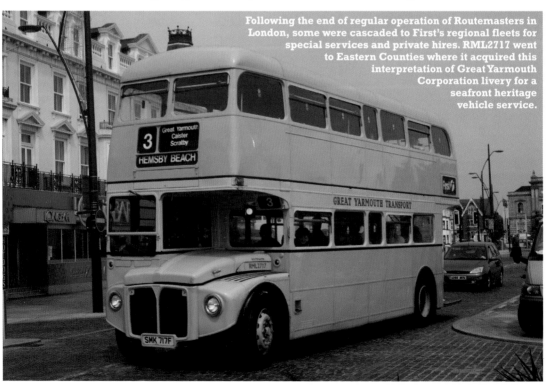

Following the end of regular operation of Routemasters in London, some were cascaded to First's regional fleets for special services and private hires. RML2717 went to Eastern Counties where it acquired this interpretation of Great Yarmouth Corporation livery for a seafront heritage vehicle service.

One of the rear-engined Blue Bird yellow schoolbuses at an open day in Aberdeen.

The distinction, which in many fleets differentiated low-floor buses from their less accessible predecessors, was probably lost on most passengers. And in any case there were step-entrance double-deckers in Barbie livery and early low-floors in Barbie 2. Within another four years Barbie 2 was abandoned, replaced by a subtly refreshed version of the original.

VEHICLE PURCHASING

As for bus types, by 1995 Badgerline pursued a purchasing policy similar to those of Stagecoach or the old NBC: large numbers of modestly equipped workhorses largely from the same sources. The vast bulk of its bodywork came from Plaxton, most chassis from Dennis. There were Darts to cover the various sizes of midibus it required, Lances as its big single-deckers, plus Mercedes-Benz van-derived minibuses.

GRT bought proportionately fewer buses built to a much high specification intended to win passengers back from their cars. These were heavy-duty single-deckers, a mix of Mercedes-Benz O405 and Scania N113 with bodywork by Wrights (still only a small if steadily expanding presence in the market) and (on later O405s) Optare. These had double-glazing, in some cases also air conditioning.

The absence of double-deckers reflected bus industry thinking post deregulation: single-deckers were cheaper to buy and operate, and if passenger numbers increased it was always possible to increase frequencies rather than the size of buses. This was an approach that

eventually would change, though First took longer to re-embrace the double-decker than some of its peers.

First's vehicle policy was a combination of those of its component parts, but a lot of GRT thinking continued to pervade it. Wrightbus, as Wrights became, remained a key supplier, on Scania and increasingly on Volvo chassis. Interior specifications remained high, with double-glazing and increased legroom accompanying the pastel interiors, though air conditioning was soon abandoned.

GRT had bought a Mercedes-Benz O405G bendybus in 1992 and First's preference for single-deckers saw it buy 124 articulated Volvos and Scanias — 106 with Wright bodies — for operation in Leeds, Manchester, Glasgow and Southampton; many of the surviving examples gravitated on to a cross-city route in Aberdeen, while a few others ended their operational lives carrying university students in Bath and Leeds. Few cities had all the infrastructure capable of accommodating them to their full potential.

It continued to buy large numbers of by then low-floor Dennis Darts with Plaxton or Alexander bodies as well as double-deckers, which from 2003 onwards were mainly Wright-bodied Volvos. The Optare Solo took the place of the Mercedes-Benz Vario as minibus of choice, though First's enthusiasm for small buses dwindled away from the level that Badgerline had displayed into the 1990s.

With strict budgets and profit targets to be met, a policy soon emerged of concentrating the intake of

A Wright SteetCar operating the 'ftr' service on the Metro reserved track in Swansea city centre.

An Irizar PB-bodied Scania operating a London-bound Greyhound service in Portsmouth.

new vehicles into locations expected to generate the highest return on the investment, so Bradford, Leeds, York, Manchester and Glasgow did well, while the less densely populated areas served by some of the former NBC and SBG companies saw far fewer new buses. Some parts of the business went years without sight of a new vehicle, receiving what are known euphemistically as 'mid-life' vehicles to tide them over.

SLIPPING STANDARDS, GRAND GESTURES

Many subsidiaries of the large groups have occasionally been called to public inquiries by traffic commissioners alerted to apparent lapses in maintenance or service reliability. By the early 2000s, First seemed to be in the spotlight more than its peers, creating a gap between the outward image of a business whose marketing slogan was 'Transforming Travel' and what was really happening.

Grand gestures helped maintain its reputation and share value with City investors, gestures often guaranteed to make good pictures to accompany the announcement of favourable financial results.

One of these was the introduction of American-style yellow schoolbuses. In common with several of the big groups, First was expanding abroad and in 1999 made the first of a series of acquisitions in North America where the core of its business was operating iconic schoolbuses like those many of us have seen in Hollywood films.

These are built to high standards of safety and are protected by road traffic laws that, among other things, prohibit other road users from passing them while they stop to pick up or set down students.

The contrast with the UK was stark. Typical schoolbuses here tended to be old vehicles, many of them sold out of the service of major fleets and run on low-price local authority contracts, eking out their final years by carrying people's precious offspring.

Moir Lockhead argued that yellow schoolbuses could change all that and imported a trial fleet of 21 Blue Bird buses built in the United States. At the time, Blue

Bird was part of the Henlys group that also owned Plaxton. There were arguments to be won with the UK authorities in order to match our regulations with what the Americans could build and the final specification made the vehicle significantly more expensive than first intended.

First threw all the PR it could at the project, hiring former cabinet minister David Blunkett as the front man for a Yellow Schoolbus Commission intended to sell the concept to local and national government and persuade large numbers of parents to abandon the school run in their cars and trust buses — like those in the movies — to carry their children instead.

It only bought a front-engined prototype and 20 with rear engines, for small contracts in West Yorkshire, Surrey and Wrexham. It had some later success with larger numbers of Turkish-built BMCs, but the yellow schoolbus revolution never happened on the scale that First had hoped.

THE BUS THAT LOOKED LIKE A TRAM

Another grand gesture with what at first glance looked like great promise was 'ftr' — text shorthand for 'future' and First's answer to cities' clamour for new age trams.

Modern trams had returned to a few British cities in the 1990s and the Labour government elected in 1997 promised that there would be many more. Then it became scared by the escalating cost of these projects, cancelled several funding promises and urged transport authorities and operators to find a cheaper alternative.

The trick was to offer all the perceived advantages of a tram — its sleek looks, high passenger capacity, reserved right of way and ease of boarding — without the high cost of laying and maintaining the rails and overhead wires.

Convinced it had found the answer, First summoned decision makers and opinion formers to Rotherham in September 2004. The venue was the Magna Science Centre, a former steelworks transformed into a post-industrial visitor attraction, and the attraction was 'ftr', a bus-based rapid transit system that would meet this new city transport need.

There was no hardware on show that day — it had yet to be built — but there were exciting images of the tram-like Wright StreetCar, a sleek bendybus built on a modified Volvo B7LA chassis. It would have two doors, the driver — to be called a pilot — would be shut off in a separate cockpit and passengers would buy their tickets from self-service machines on the bus.

All this would be accompanied by high quality bus stops, real-time passenger information and bus lanes, reserved track and traffic signal priorities to match the speed and reliability of a tram.

The clear message then, and when the prototype StreetCar was launched at Greenwich Maritime Museum the following March, was that cities would only get StreetCars if they also delivered the supporting infrastructure.

First ordered 39 more StreetCars with the promise of at least another 60 to follow and appeared so keen

Among the more recent initiatives was the revival of 1980s PMT red and yellow livery for Gold Service premium routes in North Staffordshire, as displayed in 2015 on a Scania OmniCity of First Potteries.

to get them into service that the 'no infrastructure, no StreetCar' dictum was forgotten. Only three cities got those 39 buses and only one of them provided anything approaching the amount of highway investment needed to prove their worth.

The first — in spring 2006 — went to York, which resurfaced a suburban road and created off-highway residents' car parking to clear a decent path for them to make progress, but nothing useful in the congested centre. The next tranche went to Leeds where bus stop bays were lengthened to accommodate them.

It was left to Swansea, where the last buses were taken out of prolonged storage in 2009, to show what could be done with its Metro project, which transformed the Kingsway, a city centre dual carriageway, into two two-way roads, one for general traffic and the other for buses.

There were two other major problems. One was that the self-service fare collection was untested until the first StreetCars entered service in York and passengers queued out into the street as they waited to use the machine. Buses were delayed and conductors were recruited to collect fares, increasing operating costs even if the new employees could be called 'customer hosts' and given a customer care role as well.

The other was that the buses were heavy and had a voracious thirst for fuel, also adding to operating costs. To meet budgets, the Swansea showpiece came off on evenings and Sundays, with ordinary Dennis Darts wheeled in for those quieter hours.

York and Leeds fell out of love with their StreetCars and in 2012 enough of them were refurbished for Hyperlink, a rebranded route between Leeds and Bradford that would never have been so treated had the buses not already existed and been in need of a new role in life. Then it was announced that the Swansea fleet would be withdrawn from September 2015, victims of their higher operating costs and a couple of fatal accidents involving pedestrians on the Kingsway.

The last grand gesture came in September 2009 when First imported another of its iconic American brands to the UK. This was Greyhound, the coast-to-coast coach service woven into the very romantic fabric of the United States and Canada, which had been acquired along with Laidlaw, the continent's biggest yellow schoolbus operator.

First hoped to rival National Express and Stagecoach by bringing this well-known brand on to our motorways and launched trial routes linking London and the Hampshire coast, London and Glasgow and Cardiff with Swansea. Only the Welsh route survives, though local management is more committed to the route than the American brand.

TURNING POINT

The Laidlaw takeover was a turning point for First, which raised over £200million to buy it and plunged the group heavily into debt.

City sources had expected First to sell Greyhound — which had been through several changes of ownership before First came along — in order to fund the takeover, but unlike the other UK bus groups it was reluctant to sell underperforming or non-core businesses. Some, like the Devon & Cornwall operation, went into long-term decline for want of a new owner or more modest profit targets.

The sale of the former CentreWest operations in Orpington to Go-Ahead's Metrobus in December 2007 was the first disposal since First was created and the first since GRT sold Midland Bluebird's Oban depot in 1992.

That approach changed after Lockhead — knighted in 2008 — retired in March 2011, succeeded as chief executive by former London Underground boss Tim O'Toole, an American railwayman. He persuaded one of the co-founders of the Blazefield bus group, Giles Fearnley, to come out of early retirement to head up the bus operation, which once again calls itself First Bus, now with a space between the two words.

It was becoming clear that a new strategy was needed, as inflation-busting fares increases, service reductions and poor service quality were chasing passengers away. The relationship with local transport authorities, several of whom equated First with poor service quality, also needed to be rebuilt.

Since then, a turnaround plan has focused on winning back passengers, cutting fares and investing in new, more fuel-efficient buses built mainly by Wrightbus and Alexander Dennis. Years of top-down management is being challenged with a drive for more local autonomy, while short-term profit margins have been sacrificed in pursuit of long-term growth.

It also closed or sold some underperforming businesses in 2012/13, helping pay off some of the debt from the Laidlaw deal at a time when it was also losing several of its train franchises. Stagecoach bought its businesses in Wigan, Wirral and Chester, which included a yellow schoolbus operation (with Blue Birds) in Wrexham, and provided replacement services in North Devon after the threat of a Competition Commission inquiry killed off a planned sale. Stagecoach also expanded its presence in Northampton when First wound down operations there.

Rotala's Diamond subsidiary bought the former Midland Red North operations in Redditch and Kidderminster, while Lothian Buses provided

A new livery for some premium interurban routes on a refurbished Wright-bodied Volvo B7RLE of First Scotland East for an Edinburgh-Stirling service.

replacements when First Scotland East closed its Dalkeith depot and axed routes in Midlothian and East Lothian.

The biggest divestment of all was to pull out of London in 2013. The previous year had seen it sell the former Capital Citybus depot at Northumberland Park to Go-Ahead, which also mopped up a few routes at its Dagenham depot. The biggest deals, raising £78.5million, saw five depots and 494 buses go to Metroline (owned by Singapore-based ComfortDelGro) and three depots and another 400 buses to Transit Systems, an Australian company entering the UK for the first time.

Apart from raising much-needed cash, quitting London also helped rebalance the business, as London took a disproportionate slice of First's new vehicle investment and dictated that many surplus London buses — with special features like centre doors and ramps — were cascaded to regional fleets that would rather have vehicles tailored for their own needs.

As a result of all these changes, the UK bus fleet has fallen to 6,300, lower than at any time since early 1996, but around a third of them are no more than five years old.

Further cutbacks announced in 2015 saw the group close its depots in Hereford, Newcastle-under-Lyme and Bracknell, reducing its operations in the Midlands to three depots (Worcester, Leicester and Adderley Green) and in Berkshire to one (Slough).

While the previous decade saw First lose many experienced senior managers to rival groups — the Devon & Cornwall and Scotland East subsidiaries had a succession of short-term managing directors — the new team has succeeded in attracting experienced managers, a few of whom have returned from elsewhere.

There also have been changes of livery. A refreshed version of the corporate colours was unveiled at the beginning of 2012 with more prominent local branding, and several variations have also been developed in different parts of the country.

While most of these retained some clear links to First's group identity, in early 2014 it developed The Buses of Somerset as a separate identity for routes operated out of depots in Taunton and Bridgwater, with a two-tone green livery by Best Impressions. This makes no reference to First, as an experiment to see whether it can recover lost goodwill and build new growth with a completely new brand more akin to a small independent's.

Elsewhere in south-west England, it began rebuilding lost business in Cornwall and stepped in at short notice when Western Greyhound — its principal competitor, owned until a short time before by ex-First managers — ceased trading at the end of March 2015.

These certainly are signs of big changes in how First operates. Time will tell whether they also offer evidence of a long-term recovery to deliver the promise being offered in 1995. ∎

Gricer? Twitcher? Rambler?

Chris Drew combines bus photography with other interests, which at times takes him off the beaten track.

All photographs by the author

Are gricer, twitcher and rambler affectionate names? Depends what side of the fence you are sitting on. Then there's the dreaded word that covers them all: anorak. One meaning is someone who is happy to let their hobby take over their lives completely. They can eat, drink and sleep it!

I'm sure there have been times in most people's lives when an interest, hobby, call it what you will, has seemed far more appealing than the routine of everyday life. I don't want to analyse it too much but I guess that if your life is lived in a balanced way, then it should be perfectly possible to dip in and out of a subject, putting in and taking out what you need. I chose these three subjects – buses, bird-watching and rambling - because I dip in and out of all of them, sometimes singly, sometimes more than one. They can and do overlap and complement each other.

↑WALNEY ISLAND

Here's a case in point. Walney Island is off the coast of Cumbria near Barrow-in-Furness. From the town centre in Barrow, catch Stagecoach route 1 or 1A across the Jubilee Bridge onto Walney. Both routes terminate in the South Walney area. That's the gricer element out of the way. Part two. Where I'm going is still several miles walk away and at the right time of year, they are very pleasant miles. The rambler part leads me to the largest colony of ground nesting gulls in Europe. The reserve holds some 60,000 pairs of lesser black backs and herring gulls. All bases covered. Much quieter was Barrow's 105, a Leyland Titan PD2A/27 with Massey bodywork, built in 1961 when it was numbered 5 and caught by my camera some fifteen years later in the town centre on a turn to the dockyard. At the time it was rare to find a double-decker in what was a predominantly single-deck fleet.

➡ M40 MOTORWAY NEAR STOKENCHURCH

The M40 corridor has built up to be one of the busiest commuter routes into the London area. Coach operation to and from Oxford is one of the successes of the deregulation era. Timetables, fares and vehicles have all been structured in such a way as to make the journey far more welcoming and less financially taxing than either of the alternatives on offer. At the busiest times of the day, coaches can be only minutes apart and still have good loads.

What I did find strange at first was an odd stop just off the motorway at Lewknor. This seemingly out of the way place attracts custom well into the wee small hours of the morning. That same stop offers you the spectacle of one of the UK's birding successes. Anyone who knows the area will tell you that this is where the M40 plunges downhill out of a huge cutting in the Chilterns. Even non-birders will have noticed over the past decades the silhouettes of large birds with forked tails playing on the updraught rising from the cutting. These are red kites and offer travellers on the motorway some of the best views of a bird of prey they will ever get. Nowadays large picture windows offer commuters good views of the birds as coaches thunder back and forth. Just about reaching the top of the climb is Oxford Bus Company 98, a Plaxton Panther-bodied Volvo B12B. When the M40 through the cutting was opened, the generation of vehicles found on the motorway at the time were still of the A-road era and this hill was a killer. It was not unusual to find a coach or lorry pulled over on the hard shoulder near the top, waiting for the temperature gauge to go down.

⬇ RAINHAM MARSHES

Rainham Marshes are on the north bank of the Thames just upriver from the Dartford crossing, squeezed between high tide and the high-speed rail line that carries the Eurostar on its way to Folkstone and beyond. The land once belonged to the Ministry of Defence and some structures are still in place. All manner of animal life comes through. Terns and cormorants on their way in from the estuary are common. Dolphins have been spotted on one occasion. My personal favourites are the lapwings whose courting flights make one stand and watch in awe.

So where's the bus in this one you ask? Just across the rail lines is one of the biggest used bus dealers in the country, Ensign, usually with lots of ex-Stagecoach stuff in various versions of house livery. Not that I was trying to make it difficult for myself,

but I couldn't help trying to make a Javelin sandwich as they as the trains closed at nearly 200mph with a Stagecoach bus just visible as the filling!

⬇ AVIEMORE

Aviemore is well-known as a centre for walkers, climbers and birders. Gricers seem to come a long way down the list. I didn't see another camera pointed in anger the whole week I was there. A few odd looks from passers-by though, when I lifted mine.

For birds? There is Loch Garten a few miles away. This is the ancestral home of ospreys in Scotland but to my mind, not the best place to see them.

Further on is the Findhorn Valley where, although not promised, the chances of seeing golden eagles are good. You may have gathered by now that I like raptors.

For buses? There's a small yard on the northern side of the main drag in Aviemore which is the ancestral home of the local bus company but to my mind, not the best place to see them. Further on is the station where although not promised, at the time of my visit the chances of seeing Lynxes and Ailsas was supposed to be good. There were even some VRTs. There was also a small flock of B10Ms wheeling around. You may have gathered by now, I liked Rapsons, too.

⬆ SOMERSET LEVELS

Mystical land of story and legend. That's the Somerset Levels. There are even places where the trees bow as you pass them by. That bit is actually true. Because of the watery nature of the Levels, any weight can make the surface bend enough to make the trees lean towards you. It's a bit scary to start with but you get used to it. Out of the 250 square miles called the Levels, only 500 acres remain in their original state. The rest has been put to the plough because it's so fertile. One of the most productive sites for birds is the southern edge

of West Sedgemoor where there is a wooded area. Here can be heard nightingale and the sight of a barn owl is not unusual late on into the long lingering dusks of summer. The area around the towns of Wells, Glastonbury and Street is well supplied with bus services and are close enough to be walked in a reasonable time. Things have changed some since Bristol's MW 2620 was on the road. A service like this would more than likely be operated by a huge monster of a bus dressed in lilac but not seating many, if any, more than the 43 of the MW.

CANTERBURY WOODS

First you find a friendly hostel that is willing to sell you good beer or a fine wine. Then consume said liquids for a few hours whilst passing the time playing skittles or dominoes on this warm summer evening. About an hour before dusk start walking up the Whitstable Road to the north west of town, looking for signs to Rough Common. Alternatively, catch the 27 bus and ask for the woods (spooky). When you get there you may be lucky to hear a sound you may think is a frog. You may be extremely lucky and catch sight of the silhouette of a bird with a strange flight. You may have just seen a nightjar flitting across the sun's last rays as it sets. Or, of course, you could have had one drink to many and find yourself on this East Kent Marshall-bodied AEC Swift wondering if it really was meant to be going through that archway.

LINDISFARNE

Lindisfarne is just one part of a coastline, any part of which has interest for the gricer, twitcher, or rambler. Have you ever sailed out of Seahouses looking in sheer amazement at the number of sea birds that settle a beak's distance apart on every part of the Farne Islands? Have you ever been caught by the rising tide and spent a night asleep on the beach on Holy Island? Ever seen the castle at Bamburgh towering out of a fog bank looking for all the world like it's floating in mid air? Have you ever caught the bus from Newcastle to Berwick and watched the swans come back up the Tweed in single file to roost? Warkworth was my place to roost. United Auto would supply the buses, often in the guise of an elderly Bristol RELL6G like 4120 (AHN 620B), and the double-forked Coquet Estuary would supply eider ducks, floating in rafts and giving a gentle, surprised sound amongst themselves.

BODMIN MOOR

Out on the wilds of the moor, all is quiet and tranquil. Sitting on the verge contemplating how much further till my next stop, I lie back and feel the prickle of greenery on the back of my neck. I expect to hear the mew of a buzzard whilst rising on a thermal. I might see a stonechat nipping between the tops of the gorse bushes. But wait.... a strange but somehow familiar sound comes to me from the far distance. I look, I see the top deck of a bus over the top of the hedge.

It's green all right but it's the wrong shape. It comes closer and shows itself to be an ex-East Yorkshire AEC Renown, Beverly Bar roof and all. It grinds its way towards me and I don't think I've ever heard an AEC work harder. I look for signs of ownership but none can I find. There was however, a strange hand written number in the blind box. Schools service? Workman's? My shutter releases, I raise a hand in greeting to the driver. The engine noise is soon overtaken by nature's chorus and I lay back down and go back to listening.

⬇ BREYDON WATER

A few miles inland from Great Yarmouth on the county border is a dish best served cold. And boy, does it get cold here during the winter. Nothing stops the wind straight off the North Sea. It's time to don the thick socks and Icelandic sweater. Grab a Thermos of steaming soup and be prepared to see such delights as marsh or hen harriers, merlins and short-eared owls. You might even see a rough-legged buzzard. After a few hours of that you are more than ready to rush into Great Yarmouth where you could have once seen Daimler Freelines like 18 (AEX 18B) with its dual-purpose Roe bodywork.

➡ SNOWDONIA

Snowdonia is an area of North Wales roughly defined as a rectangle joining Conwy, Betws-y-coed, Porthmadog and Caernarfon. Within these boundaries can be found many vantage points for birding, walking and bussing. One of my favourite places for all three is the pass to the south-west of Snowdon around Rhyd-Ddu. Early morning and late evening are the best times and if you're very lucky, like I was in August 2005, the sun will be out. From one spot I could see, to my left and down, a heron silently stalking something to eat. Also left but much, much higher up and crystal clear, the station at the top of Snowdon. Then, straight ahead, a Dennis Dart belonging to KMP of Llanberis making me scramble off the road as soon as the shutter was released!

⬆ POOLE HARBOUR

Poole Harbour is known as a Mecca for all sorts of pastimes. Within the area of this huge natural harbour can be found many different habitats which means that birds such as the Dartford warbler can be seen a short distance away from a water rail. The Little Sea area means a good selection of water fowl all year round, and then there's Brownsea Island on which the National Trust has worked hard to attract both birds and watchers. You will also find red squirrels on the island. Lastly, Studland, which can boast not only all six types of reptile that live in the UK but also the sometimes sunburnt or spotted nudist which are usually found at the most inopportune time! After all that, can there be anything left I hear you ask? How about a chain ferry which crosses the narrow entrance to the harbour between the two spits of Sandbanks and Studland. This also carries a bus service operated (at the time of photography) by Hants & Dorset This involved a fleet of Bristol LL6B re-bodied and modernized to gain the correct clearances when boarding the ferries. Probably I'm going to commit heresy in someone's eyes but I was very drawn to a small group of Bristol MWs, like 873, once coaches but by then comfortable buses. Nowadays, during the summer months you can catch an open-top double-decker on this journey, adding a little spice to the ferry trip.

⬆ SYMONDS YAT

Not sure what a Yat is exactly. Neither do I know who Symonds was. The Wye Valley can be classed as one of the most beautiful of its type. Just up river from Monmouth where the B4432 crosses is Symonds Yat. On the Yat Rock can be found peregrines, but down on the river itself are birds that spend much of their lives under water. These are called dippers which by a strange coincidence is one of the names which was never used (to date) by any bus company for its minibus services. Seen in 1970 at the Yat was one of Black & White's Plaxton-bodied Daimler Roadliners. Not one of their better choices I hear you say. That's as may be, but on this day UAD 315H was part of a fleet of Black & White coaches that picked up the contents of a British Rail train at Gloucester. As part of a Mystery Tour, we were transported across the Severn Bridge and up the Wye Valley.

⬇ SERVICE AREA

A motorway service area, anywhere in the UK. If you are a user of the motorway system in this country, you will have pulled into a services at sometime. There is one bird that is almost guaranteed to appear, the pied wagtail. Its darting run and bobbing tail make it easy to pick out. While I saw some at this nondescript services, my interest was taken by this ex-Western SMT Burlingham-bodied Leyland PD3 in the unusual position of being fed by hand at public pump. ∎

Independents in Greater Manchester

Small operators appeared all over Greater Manchester in the years following local bus deregulation. **Cliff Beeton** looks at some of the significant players.

All photographs by the author.

Before local bus deregulation in 1986, the Greater Manchester Passenger Transport Executive provided 95 per cent of the bus services in the region, the only notable independent operator being A Mayne and Sons which had been operating co-ordinated services with the PTE and its predecessor, Manchester City Transport, since 1930.

Shortly before deregulation the PTE formed Greater Manchester Buses, as a so-called arm's length company, to compete in the open market in the new competitive era. But after registering the services it would operate commercially and then adding those which it won by competitive tender, it was obvious that GM Buses would require 450 fewer vehicles than the PTE had owned. These surplus buses were

sold on the open market with some, ironically, going to new local independent operators who then used them on services competing with GM Buses.

The independents had lower overheads than GM Buses, and all of a sudden many small operators sprung up, some good, some bad, some just operating tendered services, others running daytime services commercially to compete with GM Buses on its busiest routes.

This allowed the independents to get a foothold in the area, and by the end of 1988 GM Buses was only operating 67 per cent of the mileage in the GMPTE area, with 63 other operators running the rest.

At the end of 1993, with privatisation looming, GM Buses was split into two units, GM Buses North and GM Buses South; both were subsequently sold in

For many years Mayne was the only independent serving central Manchester. It thrived after deregulation and its many new purchases in the 1990s included five Marshall-bodied Dennis Darts in 1998. One is followed by a Stagecoach Volvo B10M at Parrs Wood in April 2002.

management buyouts in March 1994. However finance was tight and neither company could afford to buy the large numbers of new buses needed to replace ageing fleets or to purchase competing small operators. This would change in 1996 when both were sold to large groups, GM Buses North to FirstGroup and GM Buses South to Stagecoach.

First and Stagecoach quickly began investing in much-needed new buses, and attention then turned to mopping up the local independents, so that by 2015 only a handful remained. A consequence of this policy was both groups operating services outside their traditional north/south boundaries.

Established independent Mayne, based in Clayton, operated from Ashton-under-Lyne and Droylsden to Manchester Stevenson Square, latterly with AEC Regents, Daimler Fleetlines and Bristol VRTs all bought new. Originally the company used a maroon and blue livery. This changed to maroon and cream with the arrival of the VRTs. Mayne expanded into the Tameside area to the east of Manchester in June 1986 just before deregulation, first with second-hand and later with brand new vehicles. Single-deck buses also made an appearance in the fleet. Large numbers of Scania double-deckers bodied by East Lancs and Northern Counties were purchased new in the 1990s, along with some second-hand examples from Brighton and Hove. Later low-floor buses were Dennis Tridents with East

Timeline inherited from Shearings this Leyland Tiger with Alexander Belfast bodywork, an unusual choice for an English operator. Timeline retained the Shearings livery. New in 1988, it is seen in Stockport in the summer of 1994.

Lancs and Plaxton President bodies. The bus services were sold to Stagecoach Manchester in 2008, with Mayne continuing as a coach operator.

Pennine Blue of Denton ran an immaculate blue and cream fleet of ageing Bristol RE and Leyland National single-deckers on routes around Ashton-under-Lyme. Double-deckers later appeared in the fleet. An Optare MetroRider was purchased new in 1992.The company was sold to PMT in 1993, later adopting PMT's red and yellow livery and shortening the fleetname to just

South Lancs Travel operated this ex-Timeline Tiger. The Alexander Belfast body seated 55. It was new to Shearings in 1989, and was photographed in Leigh in April 2002.

Among the double-deckers operated by Blue Bus was this former Metrobus DAF 250 with Northern Counties Palatine II body, photographed in Bolton in August 1999.

Pennine. In 2001 Pennine came under the wing of First Manchester.

Citibus Tours actually started running just before deregulation with a fleet of Leyland Panthers, ex-Great Yarmouth AEC Swifts and an ex-Newport Metro Scania in an attractive light blue and black livery on routes between Manchester and Blackley. Leyland Nationals and double-deckers appeared later. The firm was acquired by Lynton Travel who later sold it to GM Buses North.

Dennis of Dukinfield started operating between Manchester and Ashton with Mercedes minibuses and an Optare Delta purchased new, using a red and light grey livery. Leyland Nationals appeared before low-floor Dennis Tridents and Darts became the fleet standards. The first low-floor Dennis Trident appeared in red and yellow, but with Pennine adopting those colours the company reverted to red and grey. The business was sold to Stagecoach Manchester in 2009.

Finglands was one of many operators which bought ex-GMPTE Fleetlines and Atlanteans to operate services in the Greater Manchester area. This is a Northern Counties-bodied Leyland Atlantean.

Blue Bus of Horwich was formed in 1991 by two former Shearings managers, and operated around the Bolton area with second-hand Leyland Leopards and Atlanteans in an attractive two-tone blue and cream livery. It went on to purchase many new vehicles with the livery being changed to a two-tone blue scheme. Vehicles purchased new included batches of Plaxton Pointer Darts, Ikarus and Wright Cadet-bodied DAFs and the first MAN 14.220 chassis with East Lancs Myllennium bodywork. Double-deckers included East Lancs Olympians and Plaxton President-bodied Dennis Tridents. Low-floor buses were marketed as Blue Buggy Bus.

The Bolton operations of Blazefield's Lancashire United were acquired in 2002. In 2005 Blue Bus sold its Appley Bridge operation to South Lancs Travel and later in the year the remainder of the business was sold to Arriva North West.

Shearings was a coach operator which was successful in winning tendered services from the PTE at deregulation, particularly around the Bolton and Bury areas. To service these a fleet of second-hand Leyland Nationals was acquired. These were followed by two batches of Leyland Lynxes bought new. Further new buses included unusual Leyland Tigers and Volvo B10Ms with Alexander Belfast bodies, as Shearings built up one of the most modern bus fleets in the area.

When the Rank group took over Shearings' parent company, Mecca, in 1990, a policy change was to concentrate on coaching and sell the bus operations. These were sold to a management buyout in 1991, and the business was renamed Timeline but kept the same yellow, cream and orange livery. Timeline continued to invest in new vehicles with Mercedes minibuses, Alexander Dash-bodied Dennis Darts and Optare Excels. The Greater Manchester operations were sold to First Manchester in 1998.

Bullocks of Cheadle was another coach operator tempted into bus operations at deregulation, with second-hand Fleetlines from London, GMPTE and other sources working around Stockport and the lucrative Wilmslow Road corridor into Manchester. Some single-deckers, including ex-PMT Leyland National 2s, appeared before newer ex-Southampton Dennis Dominators arrived. New vehicles included dealer stock Volvo Olympians and the first low-floor buses in Manchester, two Optare Spectras in 1998. Later new low-floor double-deckers included East Lancs-bodied Scanias and Dennis Tridents.

Most of the bus services were sold to Stagecoach Manchester in August 2008. In 2015 the only route operated by Bullocks is the 147 from Manchester

Walls was another operator to use ex-GMPTE buses on new services in the late 1980s. This one is a Daimler Fleetline with Northern Counties bodywork, photographed at East Didsbury in 1994.

An unusual bus in the Tame Valley fleet was this Alexander-bodied Ailsa which had been new to the West Midlands PTE and later operated for London Buses and Taylor of Morley, making it not second-hand but fourth-hand. Ailsas were never a common type in Greater Manchester.

UK North operated a varied fleet with varied maintenance standards, which included this smart-looking DAF SB220 with Ikarus body. It is at Hazel Grove, ready for the 10-mile trip on the 192 service to Manchester Piccadilly.

Promoted as the first low-floor double-deckers in Manchester were a pair of Optare Spectras in the Bullocks fleet. The Spectra was built on the DAF DB250 chassis. This one is seen when new in May 1999.

Piccadilly to the University area using four Wrightbus-bodied Volvo B5LH hybrid double-deckers.

Finglands was a coach operator based on the Wilmslow Road that had started operating contract services for students from Owens Park to the University in the 1980s, so it was not surprising that it introduced regular bus services on this lucrative corridor in1986. A fleet of ex-GMPTE Leyland Atlanteans and Daimler Fleetlines was obtained and painted in a brown, orange and cream livery. Later arrivals included ex-London Buses MkII Metrobuses. A brand new Alexander-bodied Volvo Citybus was purchased in 1989.

Finglands was sold to East Yorkshire in 1992 but continued as a separate unit, keeping its existing livery. New buses entered the fleet after this, and in 1994 Finglands purchased the fledgling Stagecoach Manchester operation working the 192 from Hazel Grove to Manchester, a move which cleared the way for Stagecoach to buy GM Buses South from its management. In 2014 East Yorkshire sold the bus services to First Manchester, with the coaches going to Bullocks.

Walls Coaches started running buses on the Wilmslow Road corridor at deregulation with second-hand Bristol VRTs and ex-GMPTE Daimler Fleetlines in an attractive green and white livery. It went on to purchase brand new DAF SB220s with Optare and Ikarus bodywork

as well as Northern Counties Palatine II-bodied DAF double-deckers giving Walls one of the most modern bus fleets in the city. The bus operations were sold to Stagecoach Manchester in 1997.

Bluebird of Middleton was originally a coach operator that expanded into buses in 1988 building up a modern fleet in a two-tone blue livery. Dennis Darts and Enviro200s formed the backbone of the fleet. Routes from Middleton to Manchester were later expanded to include Oldham area services. In March 2013 the company was sold to Stagecoach Manchester.

Stuarts of Hyde started bus operations in 1987 working into Manchester from the Hyde area using ex-West Midlands PTE Daimler Fleetlines and Leyland Atlanteans from various sources in a white livery with green, yellow and red patches. New buses in the form of Ikarus-bodied DAF SB220s with their unusual route number blinds with black numbers on white backgrounds appeared later on, and the company

One of JP Travel's Dennis Darts with East Lancs bodywork and appropriate registration S3 JPT arrives at Piccadilly Gardens in Manchester in May 2008. The company had around two dozen JPT registration marks; S3 JPT was originally carried by a Mercedes-Benz Vario.

opened a new garage at Dukinfield. An accident involving a school bus in 1998 brought this operator to an early end.

Tame Valley was another operator to run buses in the Tameside area after deregulation using mainly ex-GMPTE Daimler Fleetlines and Leyland Nationals, operating between Hyde and Stockport in an attractive two-tone green and cream livery. The operation passed to Glossopdale in 1995. Glossopdale had started running services from Glossop to Ashton and Stockport in a white and green livery. An interesting initial vehicle was an ex-Boro'line Maidstone Wright-bodied Bedford. Later vehicles were Marshall-bodied Dennis Darts and a rare Marshall Minibus. The livery was later modified to two tone green. Glossopdale was sold to Stagecoach Manchester in 1999.

MyBus of Hadfield started running buses shortly after deregulation from Hyde to Manchester using a variety of second-hand double-deckers in a red and cream

livery. Ex-GMPTE Atlanteans and Fleetlines shared the duties with former London Transport B20 Fleetlines. Maintenance issues forced the closure of the business in 1993.

UK North was a phoenix of MyBus based at Gorton which started operations in 1995, mainly on the Wilmslow Road corridor with second-hand ex-Harris Bus Leyland Olympians with East Lancs Pyoneer bodywork in a blue and red livery. New Ikarus-bodied DAF SB220s and Alexander ALX400-bodied DAF 250s suggested a bright future, but ongoing trouble with the Traffic Commissioner with maintenance and operating issues continued to affect the company. The final nail in the coffin was when a UK North double-decker hit a man working on a cherry-picker, unfortunately killing him. A subsequent enquiry by the Traffic Commissioner closed the company down.

Stotts of Oldham originally started operating contracts for the many mill workers in the Oldham area

Bluebird ran a smart fleet which included ADL Enviro200s with bodywork by Alexander or, more unusually, MCV. Eight MCV-bodied Enviro200s were delivered in 2007-08, all with BLU registrations. The company was taken over by Stagecoach in 2013.

in the 1970s. When the mills started closing down in the mid 1980s Stotts turned its hand to bus work using a variety of double-deckers in a black, red and off-white livery. Ex-GMPTE Daimler Fleetlines were later joined by ex-South Yorkshire examples. Dennis Dominators would be added later. The bus services were concentrated on the Oldham area and were sold to First Manchester in 1997.

Stotts restarted operating buses in 2003, again in the Oldham area, later expanding into Stockport on GMPTE tendered services. It is one of the few independents still running buses in Greater Manchester in 2015,with Optare Solos, Enviro200 Darts and ex-Stagecoach London Alexander ALX400-bodied Dennis Tridents.

South Lancs Travel of Atherton started out as Green Triangle with bus services around Atherton and Leigh.

The opening of the Trafford Centre prompted SLT to run services there, purchasing its first double-decker to do so. The Appley Bridge depot of Blue Bus with routes and staff was purchased in 2005. In 2011 SLT was sold to Staffordshire-based D&G Bus. The present modern fleet contains Plaxton Pointer Dennis Darts, Optare Solos and Tempos, and Wright-bodied Scanias and MANs. In February 2015 D&G sold the company to Rotala.

Jim Stones started bus operations in Leigh in 1986 and has always run immaculately-presented vehicles in a two-tone blue and white livery, with most vehicles purchased new. Initially Dennis Plaxton Mini Pointer Darts were used but these have been replaced by Enviro200 Darts. The company still owns one of the original Leyland DAB Tiger Cubs, one of only two imported into the country. Apart from the Tiger Cub all of the fleet carry cherished registrations. Jim Stones is still operating buses in 2015.

Named after the initials of founders Janet and Peter Walsh, JP Travel started bus operations in

Dennis's Dennis. Dennis's of Dukinfield bought this Dennis Trident with East Lancs bodywork new in the spring of 2003. It is seen at Ashton-under-Lyne bus station when just a few months old. It was one of five similar buses.

Universal Buses bought six UVG-bodied Dennis Darts in 1997; this one is seen in Manchester city centre in February 1998.

1987, in the Middleton area of Manchester, later expanding into the Oldham and Tameside areas and latterly to Manchester itself. The initial fleet consisted of minibuses, later progressing to Dennis Darts in an attractive yellow and blue livery. Double-deckers started to appear later. In 2007 the bus routes operated by Ashalls were taken over. Later a policy of purchasing new vehicles saw Plaxton Primos and Plaxton Centro-bodied MANs arrive; these were later joined by Enviro200 Darts and even an Enviro400 double-decker. The Enviro400 only lasted three years before being sold. A trend towards buying older second-hand vehicles then started, ironically replacing low-floor vehicles with step-entrance ones, before the company was sold to Stagecoach Manchester in April 2014.

The Lyntown Bus Company started operating from Eccles to Manchester after deregulation with a smart fleet of Bristol RE single-deckers in a livery of red, green and cream. It was taken over by Midway Motors in 1990 who changed the livery to blue, cream and yellow but had ceased trading by 1992.

Hulme Hall Coaches was founded by Hulme Hall Grammar School as a means of providing transport to the school from the surrounding area using vehicles in a smart cream and dark red livery. Initially the operation used coaches including an ex-Standerwick Bristol VRL and an MCW Metroliner double-decker before building up a fleet of Bristol VRTs, later joined by

After PMT acquired Pennine Blue in 1993 it used this attractive two-tone blue and yellow livery for a short time before adopting PMT red and yellow. The bus is a 1980 Bristol VRT transferred from the PMT fleet.

Leyland Olympians and a Leyland National Greenway. Some ex-Stagecoach Volvo B6 Alexander Dash-bodied midibuses were acquired for GMPTE-supported service 379 from Pointon to Manchester Airport and branded as Hulme Hall Buses. The company ceased trading in 2012.

Universal Buses of Littleborough, an offshoot of BuVal Buses, started running in 1998 using UVG-bodied Dennis Darts and Optare Excels in a mainly white livery between Manchester and Tameside. By 2000 it had been taken over by Stagecoach Manchester. BuVal reappeared in the mid 2000s using Dennis Mini Pointer Darts on services around Rochdale and Littleborough. The company closed in 2011. ■

Wellington Street Coach Station

It has vanished without trace but, as **Tony Greaves** illustrates, Wellington Street Coach Station in Leeds was once a hive of activity.

During my childhood when we made family visits to relatives in Pudsey, I first became aware of the coach station on Wellington Street in Leeds, which consisted of a rectangle of tarmac curiously slotted in between a row of office buildings and hemmed in on three sides by buildings. The railway station on the opposite side of Wellington Street, where London Pullman trains were to be seen, was Leeds Central station, yet the bus equivalent, Leeds Central Bus Station was and still is, on the opposite side of the city.

The Central railway station has long gone and most of the site it occupied was used for many years from the early 1970s as a summer overspill for the coach station. Despite the rough ground, some of the departure marker boards on stands were brought from over the road and used to lay the area out in some sort of order for departures. A huge assortment of independent coach operators' vehicles were to be observed on hire to West Yorkshire Road Car, mainly on East Coast duplicate workings.

These were in addition to the regular long-distance express services provided by the many colourful

The driver of dual-purpose West Yorkshire Bristol LS5G SUG37 (OWX 149) keeps the door open for a clear line of sight as he turns into Wellington Street on the long journey to Liverpool in the mid-1960s, before the M62 Trans-Pennine motorway was built. The North Western vehicle behind is operating the same service in the opposite direction, to Newcastle.

TOP RIGHT: **The conductor of East Yorkshire Leyland Titan double-deck coach 572 (MKH 81) of 1951 guides the driver into his departure slot, while a Lancashire United Leyland Tiger Cub awaits its departure for Liverpool and the United Bristol MW will head north to Middlesbrough. The end of the Leeds Central Station platform was an excellent vantage point for photography.**

MIDDLE RIGHT: **United Auto Bristol BUE601 (2601 HN), a dual-purpose MW5G built in 1960, was one of a large fleet of similar vehicles. It awaits its departure time on the X99 to Middlesbrough, 70 miles to the north.**

BELOW RIGHT: **East Yorkshire AEC Bridgemaster 756 (3756 RH) departs for Hull on the 46 service, via York and Pocklington. This is the start of the NBC era, with corporate signage to the left of the bus and a West Yorkshire dual-purpose RELL in the background. The Bridgemaster was thankfully a much more comfortable bus to ride on than it looked. The needs of waiting smokers and chocoholics were met with the provision of a kiosk, just visible on the left of the picture.**

operators whose liveries were lost upon the introduction of the National Express white identity.

For many years a consortium of operators working as the Yorkshire Pools service ran a joint express service between Liverpool and Newcastle upon Tyne; these included Lancashire United, Northern General, North Western Road Car, United Automobile, West Yorkshire and Yorkshire Woollen District. Coaches representing these companies alone were a source of great interest, as they were from British Electric Traction, Transport Holding Company and independent fleets, with all the vehicular variety expected from those operators.

East Yorkshire Motor Services operated services between the east coast and Leeds, several of which used double-deckers, ranging from the full-front Leyland PD2s with Beverley Bar roof and almost avant-garde styling, through the unfortunately-styled Bridgemasters and Renowns to lowheight Daimler Fleetlines. United Auto, which ran to Ripon, and West Yorkshire Road Car, were more predictable in their choice of coaches, these being the standard Tilling, THC or National Bus Company group fare of the time.

The deregulation of coach services in 1980 and a decline in demand for many services to the coast led to a reduction in West Yorkshire hiring in independent operators, a decline that continued after the division of West Yorkshire, and the eventual sale of the company to Yorkshire Rider in August 1989.

ABOVE: **North Western Alexander Y-type Leyland Leopard 149 (AJA 149B) has just arrived and the driver has gone for a break before the return journey to Manchester. The owner of the luggage in the foreground would not expect it to be still there on his or her return nowadays.**

The reconstruction of the Central Bus Station during the mid 1990s included a new coach station on a new access road built on the western side of the existing complex, which moved it closer to the city centre as well as increasing its size. With the opening of the new facility in 1996 Wellington Street was finally closed and a start was made on the redevelopment of the site. New offices and a new pavement have perfectly filled the vacant slot so that all traces of the coach station have gone, and no-one would know it had ever existed. ■

TOP OF PAGE: **An early morning departure for East Kent Park Royal-bodied AEC Reliance DJG 613C on its marathon journey to Dover and Folkestone, calling at Margate, Cliftonville and Ramsgate. Unusually for a big company, East Kent did not use fleet numbers at this time.**

TOP RIGHT: **Dual-purpose Northern General Alexander-bodied Leyland Leopard 2638 (FCN 638F) was in original condition some five years after delivery, complete with the yellow-on-blue destination blinds used for express services.**

MIDDLE RIGHT: **In the 1970s the summer duplicate services working on hire to West Yorkshire departed from the site vacated by the demolition of Leeds Central station. An ex-Global of London Duple Continental-bodied AEC Reliance and a Duple-bodied Bedford VAL, both from the varied fleet of Boddy's of Bridlington, prepare for their journey back to the east coast.**

BOTTOM RIGHT: **A colourful pair from up north meet at Wellington Street. United Auto Bristol RELH6G 1253 (NHN 953E) in glorious green express livery stands alongside Duple-bodied Ford NT29 (URS 629K) of Alexander Northern, which was a long way from its Aberdeen base.**

There's slight embarrassment as passengers and staff help to start a loaded ex-East Yorkshire Harrington-bodied Tiger Cub of Eddie Brown Tours, to the amusement of onlookers.

LEFT: **Representing its participation in the Yorkshire Pool service East Yorkshire Leyland Panther 798 (GAT 798D) with dual-purpose seating in its Marshall body is about to depart for Blackpool. It wears a more complex than usual version of indigo and primrose bus livery, despite being fitted with coach-type seating.**

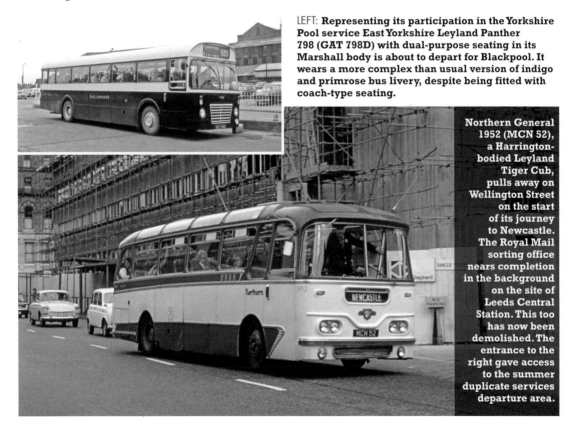

Northern General 1952 (MCN 52), a Harrington-bodied Leyland Tiger Cub, pulls away on Wellington Street on the start of its journey to Newcastle. The Royal Mail sorting office nears completion in the background on the site of Leeds Central Station. This too has now been demolished. The entrance to the right gave access to the summer duplicate services departure area.

LEFT: **Ribble 307 (LRN 307J), a 1971 Marshall-bodied Bristol RESL6L, awaits departure for Blackpool on the overspill site. It features the modernised fleetname adopted in 1968, but offers little comfort with 47 bus seats for the 75-mile journey.**

BELOW: **In Leeds City Square, within half a mile of the coach station, is one of East Yorkshire's pair of Leyland Panther coaches with Metro-Cammell Topaz bodies. The order was originally placed with Weymann but had to be re-directed when the company suffered a factory fire. As built, they were handsome, almost exotic-looking coaches in primrose and Riviera blue, but as seen here, they were rebuilt using some Plaxton parts that didn't sit well with the original.**

A surprise participant on the London service in early 1974 was the unique integral Scania CR145 with rear-mounted 14.2-litre V8 engine, promoted as the MCW 145. The front seat ride was as impressive as expected, as compared with the standard coaches of the era with leaf springs and underfloor engines.

A West Yorkshire Plaxton Paramount 4000, one of four in the fleet for Rapide services, departs for London with a West Riding Alexander TE-bodied Leyland Tiger and a United Plaxton-bodied Leyland Leopard in the background. These National Express double-deck Paramounts, with Gardner 6LYT engines, were based on Neoplan N722/3 underframes and were built at a time when Neoplan would produce virtually anything a customer wanted.

Lincoln City Transport operated vehicles such as this Volvo B10M double-deck with an East Lancs body on the 381, from Lincoln to Blackpool, via Leeds, Bradford, Keighley, Burnley, Accrington, Blackburn and Preston. For some that may be a little too much for the 'Nice Day' message offered in the destination display.

London's
UNIQUE DOUBLE-DECKER

There may be conflicting views on the benefits of London's New Routemaster, but **Michael Baker** is a fan. He takes a look at this unique vehicle.

E very so often something happens in the bus world which takes just about everyone completely by surprise. Such an event was the introduction into service of the New Bus for London, the New Routemaster, the LT, on 2 April 2012.

Perceived opinion from the earliest days of the motorbus right through to the original Routemaster was that operating conditions in London were so different from any other urban environment that a special design of double-decker was needed to cope with them. However the world was changing. Production of the Routemaster ended in 1968,

London Transport lost its Country Area operations to the National Bus Company two years later, and as we moved into the 1970s, the confidence which had once characterised those in charge of public transport in London seemed to evaporate.

Politics, and party politics in particular, which had always played a significant part, seemed to override all other considerations. Ken Livingstone as Labour leader of the Greater London Council became involved in an unedifying if sometimes amusing slanging match with Conservative prime minister Margaret Thatcher, and a series of disastrous ventures into modified versions of standard designs

A working prototype of the New Bus for London was tested at the Millbrook proving ground in Bedfordshire in the summer of 2011. TfL

of rear-engined single- and double deck-buses brought the reputation of London Transport to an all-time low.

The absorption of AEC, the traditional supplier of London buses, into the Leyland empire had done nothing to improve its viability, The failure of the AEC Merlin single-decker, some examples of which had to be taken out of service within four years and sent straight to the scrapyard, meant this once fine manufacturer which had supplied vehicles all over the world as well as to London, disappeared into oblivion.

A mock-up of the completed vehicle was exhibited at the London Transport Museum in 2011, alongside earlier generations of purpose-designed London buses. The 12-series registration plate was presumably indicative of Transport for London's 2012 target date for the vehicle's introduction. STEWART J. BROWN

Time, and politics, moved on. London acquired a mayor with considerable powers, Ken Livingstone being the first. He was succeeded in 2008 by Boris Johnson, and one of his election pledges was that he would bring back a bus specially designed for London. This generated a mixture of snorts of derision and a chorus of scoffs from, if not quite all and sundry, certainly a wide spectrum of the great and good experts who knew better. Whatever one thinks of Boris's politics, he does have a great deal of charisma, and as a darling of the media, a remarkable ability to get his own way.

A competition was announced in July 2008 for a bus which, Johnson declared, would be 'stylish, spacious and energy efficient'. The extraordinary total of around 700 entries was received, some from children for which there was a special category. There were still plenty of doubters but, undaunted, a short list of just two manufacturers was arrived at, Alexander Dennis and Wrightbus of Ballymena. On 23 December 2009 Wrightbus was announced as the winner, and at the beginning of 2010 the Heatherwick design studio was brought in to work with the Northern Irish firm.

This combination was a truly fascinating coming together of youth and maturity, for Thomas Heatherwick was 39 years old, William Wright 81. William had joined his father's coachbuilding firm shortly after the end of World War 2, and would become its driving force. Although he gave up as chairman in 2001, handing over to his son, Jeff, it

Production model LT61 (LTZ 1061), operated by London General, loads at Aldwych in January 2015. MICHAEL BAKER

A pair of London General New Routemasters head along Whitehall on the 453, which for a time was operated by Mercedes-Benz Citaro artics. MICHAEL BAKER

London United operates New Routemasters on three routes including the 148 between White City and Camberwell Green. MICHAEL BAKER

was obvious when I visited him at the Wrightbus factory in December 2014 that William, who was awarded the OBE in 2009 for his business acumen and an honorary Doctor of Science degree by the University of Ulster, was still totally involved in the firm. Thomas Heatherwick, OBE, is a brilliant designer, a graduate of the Royal College of Art, best known possibly for the Olympic cauldron featured at the opening ceremony of the London Olympics, and the new garden bridge which is to be built across the Thames. With that sort of parentage the new London bus could hardly help being something out of the ordinary and so it proved.

Wright had entered the London bus market fairly late on, its first London deliveries being on Mercedes-Benz 811Ds and Renault S75s in 1989-90. But despite being based across the water in Ireland the company competed successfully with its English and Scottish rivals, rapidly establishing a reputation both for reliability and innovation.

Heatherwick took the approach that, having never designed a bus before, whilst bearing in mind the traditions of the Routemaster and its predecessors, it would go back to a complete rethink of what a double-deck bus serving central London should be.

By November, 2010 a full size mock up was ready and my wife, Maeve, and I were given a tour of it when it was put on display at London Transport Museum's Acton depot. It did not disappoint. Undoubtedly the most controversial feature was the open rear platform, complete with conductor.

Before I could ask our guide commented: 'I know, I know, health and safety. The Department for Transport could find no statistics regarding accidents, so few were they in the days of Routemaster operation in central London, and we were given the go-ahead.'

Heatherwick's attitude to the rear staircase – there is also one at the front – was that if we've got one let's celebrate it and consequently much of the rear is glazed and from certain angles, particularly at night, it really does look as if the New Bus for London has an open staircase just like buses of the 1920s. It is no coincidence that after much deliberation the bus was designated LT although the press and the public insisted on calling it the New Routemaster and Transport for London accepted the inevitable and have adopted this title too. The mock-up was later

LT150 (LTZ 1150) was delivered in the spring of 2014 wearing a silver livery to support Transport for London's Year of the Bus. MICHAEL BAKER

put on display at the London Transport Museum at Covent Garden where, again, it was much admired. With very little modification the next stage was a working prototype.

This went on test at the Millbrook test track in Bedfordshire in June 2011. The first complete working bus was unveiled at Ballymena in November of that year, shipped across a few days later and on 16 December became the first New Bus for London to appear on the streets of the capital, launched to the

A few New Routemasters have carried advertising liveries. Metroline LT99 (LTZ 1099) was promoting Android in the early months of 2015. MICHAEL BAKER

A Wrightbus comparison, with a 2012 Volvo B9TL with Eclipse Gemini body following LT106 (LTZ 1106) as they head towards Euston Road in the summer of 2014. Both buses are in the Metroline fleet. STEWART J. BROWN

sort of press reception normally reserved for a soap star announcing that she and her husband of two weeks have agreed to an amicable separation. Boris Johnson was not, of course, exactly hiding behind the back of the bus. He actually drove it outside City Hall, handing over to Leon Daniels, TfL managing director surface transport, who in turn handed over to Sir Peter

Hendy, TfL transport commissioner - both of whom are true enthusiasts and can often be seen at rallies driving Sir Peter's preserved Routemaster.

Autocar, a magazine not normally given to bus reviews, understandably concentrated on what the new bus was like to drive. 'Seated in the widely adjustable but pretty flat driver's seat you get a supremely clear view forward….as you ease off the brake pedal the NBfL creeps forward with eerie smoothness. Never before has a hybrid drive train seemed so suited to a vehicle. Get into a groove and there's a real pleasure to be had from driving the NBfL smoothly and placing it accurately – even more so because the power delivery is so smooth: it's public transport as it should be.'

The New Routemaster is 11.2 metres long, weighs 12 tonnes, has a maximum speed of 50mph, and can carry 87 passengers, 40 seated upstairs, 22 seated downstairs and 25 standing. Powered by green diesel-electric hybrid technology it is noticeably quieter than some of its predecessors. Indeed one can be sitting inside as it loads up and suddenly think, 'Goodness me, the engine has cut out,' only to realise that this is what it is supposed to do as it moves off virtually silently.

An order was placed for 600, and the first to enter normal service was LT2 which took up work on 27 February 2012 from Ash Grove garage on route 38. This was particularly appropriate for this had long been a haunt of the original Routemaster, and there had been a great outcry from passengers when these were replaced by the unloved Mercedes-Benz Citaro bendybuses.

I had my first ride a short while later, which involved a considerable wait and detective work tracking it down as LT2 remained the sole representative of this new era right through March, LT1 joining it early in April. By July the first eight had arrived and the LT was becoming a familiar sight around Hyde Park Corner and in Piccadilly, although all eight were seldom at work together as the first two went off on a world tour and various members were required at rallies and publicity events.

The public took the LT to its heart right from the start but especially when route 24 from Pimlico to Hampstead Heath became the first to be worked entirely by the type on 22 June 2013. Posters had been put up along the route advertising the new buses and it wasn't just enthusiasts who were out and about; indeed they were very much in the minority as the public was out in force. A busy route at any time, on that day the 24 was simply swamped with passengers. I boarded at Pimlico and within three stops there was standing room only. Heads turned as we went past, mobile phones suddenly appeared and their cameras were clicked at us and one overheard enthusiastic comments.

The conductor is there basically to check that all is well with passengers alighting and boarding on the rear platform, although they also check, but don't provide, tickets. Once the evening rush hour is over they depart and the rear doors are closed off, although, of course they are opened and closed by the driver at stops, just like the front and middle doors.

So is this wonderful bus totally without fault? Well, since you ask, no. When TfL announced in the summer of 2014 that it had ordered another 200 from the Ballymena factory it also said that problems with ventilation were being addressed and remedied on the entire fleet. One hopes this is true for it was around this time on a hot summer afternoon that I boarded a 24 near Euston, climbed to the upper deck, and found conditions far from comfortable. The bus was hot. Passengers were complaining to each other, and the young man in front of me unscrewed a bottle of water and poured some of it down the back of his neck. Alighting near Tottenham Court Road to change to a 38 was better, but still rather uncomfortable and as other passengers boarded I heard one say, 'Oh it's one of those smelly buses.'

I wrote to TfL, pointing out that I thought that basically this was a quite splendid bus but that there clearly was a problem with ventilation. I got a detailed reply assuring me that the problem had been recognised and that it was quite certainly being remedied. We must hope this is so. Air-conditioning on city buses in the British Isles which make frequent stops has not always been successful. One hopes technology has moved on.

Since their introduction on the 24 more and more central London routes have gone over to the New Routemaster, following the pattern of its predecessor, the RML, which in its final decades was concentrated on those routes passing through the heart of the West End – Oxford Street in particular – and the City, as did its predecessor, the RTW, London's first 8ft-wide motor bus.

In the spring of 2015 there were 13 routes on which LTs could be found, as shown on the accompanying table. That rose to 14 in October when Arriva's 149 (London Bridge Station to Edmonton Green) got New Routemasters. Already there are several areas in central London - Victoria Street, the Strand and Trafalgar Square, to name just three - where one may see New Routemasters, which if not totally dominating the scene are certainly heading that way.

Traditional red is the colour applied to the great majority of LTs but there have been a number of variations, mostly all-over adverts, whilst LT60 has been most fetchingly attired in a version of London General's pre 1933 red, off white and silver. It will be interesting to see what livery variations might appear later in the New Routemaster's life. ∎

Hop aboard! The rear entrance and staircase of the New Routemaster. MICHAEL BAKER

Warrington Borough Transport: THEN AND NOW

Warrington native **John Robinson** illustrates changes in his home town.

Born a Warringtonian, and living in the town until 1969, I always admired the smart red and white buses of Warrington Corporation Transport Department. Under Local Government re-organisation in April 1974 the undertaking became known as Warrington Borough Council Transport Department and later, on local bus deregulation in October 1986, Warrington Borough Transport Ltd. In 2006 the fleet was re-branded as Network Warrington, under which guise it continues to operate as one of just 11 UK council-owned bus operators.

The fleet today is highly standardised and mostly single-deck (approximately 75 per cent), a complete contrast to how it used to be; even in August 1987,

less than 12 months after deregulation, there were just five full-size operational saloons in a total fleet of 90.

Following on from my similar feature covering West Midlands PTE in *Buses Yearbook 2013*, I have selected a number of photographs I took in the 1970s and 1980s of Warrington buses and then, in 2014 and 2015, taken equivalent views at the same locations.

With the original pictures to hand for reference, where practicable I have taken the present-day photographs with the same focal length of lens from

TOP LEFT: **Daimler Fleetline 28 (BED 735C), the second of a pair new in 1965, heads into the town centre along Winwick Street in October 1979, passing Central Station on the former Cheshire Lines Committee route from Manchester to Liverpool. It has a relatively uncommon design of East Lancs bodywork which was also specified by the municipalities of Bury, Coventry and Sheffield. Sitting atop the sandstone arches, behind the Liverpool platform wall, is the former site of Warrington Central loco shed, although in reality little more than a siding. The bus displays a 9 blind for the service to the newly-developed area of Oakwood, part of the growing Warrington New Town. Because of the infrequent nature of the service, buses working it had long layovers on return to Warrington before taking up the next journey out so were sometimes used as staff runabouts, as seen here with a conductress on the platform.**

BOTTOM LEFT: **Although still recognisable, this location has undergone major transformation and the structure carrying the sidings has been rebuilt wider than previously to form part of Midland Way, an elevated road running between the east and west sides of the town centre. The Midland Hotel, just visible on the right of the original view, has now disappeared whilst the sandstone railway arches along Crown Street have been rebuilt in brick although the new road bridge abutment is sandstone, presumably reclaimed from the original structure. In April 2015 Wrightbus Eclipse Urban-bodied Volvo B7RLE 90 (DK09 ELJ), one of 12 new in 2009, turns right into Warrington Interchange, opened in 2006. This replaced the nearby Golden Square bus station, which had opened in 1979.**

TOP RIGHT: **The narrowness of the section of Sankey Street between Bold Street and Market Gate precluded the use of 8ft-wide buses and in the mid 1960s Warrington Corporation was faced with the problem of obtaining new 7ft 6in-wide buses to replace older ones. Leyland obliged by building 12 special PD2/40s to overall dimensions of 28ft 5in by 7ft 6in which arrived in 1965. Their East Lancs forward-entrance bodies, the first double-deckers of this layout in the fleet, seated 64. Ironically, the offending part of the street was made one-way in an eastbound direction in February 1966, making it possible for all types of bus to use it. 49 (BED 730C) heads out of town along Dial Street in August 1975 on service 2 from Dallam to Fisher Avenue, Orford. The tower crane in the background presages early work in the town centre re-development and the building of the Golden Square shopping centre.**

BOTTOM RIGHT: **Dial Street is now the main road out of the town centre for bus services heading in the direction of Manchester Road. Volvo B7RLE/Wrightbus 88 (DK09 ELH) operates service 4A to Woolston in April 2015. The road here is now re-aligned and heavily tree-lined but the old building on the left, originally the Warrington Savings Bank, built in 1817, confirms the location. Also still there is the building to the immediate right of the bus, which is Vigo House, the home of Warrington Conservative Club. Alongside is part of Ampleforth House, new housing designed to a traditional style.**

what I believe to be exactly the same position. This is achieved by ensuring that intersecting angles, such as roof lines, chimneys and windows appear in exactly the same relative positions in each pair of photographs. However, at some locations the subsequent re-alignment of roads or a proliferation of street furniture has dictated a slightly different position. Also, in some cases, I've shot slightly wider than originally in order to put the location into context or to improve the composition.

The original photographs were taken with film cameras (both 35mm and a 120 Rolleicord) using standard lenses so it has been easy to replicate the same settings for the modern day pictures, taken with a digital camera.

I have featured locations where there are common elements in both pictures; in many locations, particularly in and around the town centre, the entire topography has altered as development has taken place. In such locations, with not even a single

reference point to act as a visual anchor to the past view it would be difficult, if not impossible, to determine or access the spot the original picture was taken from and, even if this was possible, without any linking features the impact of a comparison shot would be lost.

The choice of views has largely been dictated by the availability of suitable historic images, together with the continued presence of buses at previously-photographed locations, so is not intended to reflect a broad spread of vehicle types or locations within the company's operating area. Nonetheless, I have attempted to maximise diversity across both these aspects, which has necessitated featuring, in some of the present views, operators other than Warrington Borough Transport.

The pictures broadly start in Warrington town centre and work outwards to the farthest location featured, the A49 swing bridge over the Weaver Navigation, around nine miles away. ■

Following a three-week visit by Daimler Fleetline demonstrator 7000 HP in March 1962, Warrington became an early purchaser of the model when nine, bodied by East Lancs, arrived towards the end of 1963. Heading out of Sankey Street into Liverpool Road on service 2A to Dallam in February 1980 is 24 (5833 ED). Bank Park, opened to the public in 1873, and the Town Hall grounds are visible on the left.

East Lancs-bodied 73 (LED 73P), numerically the last Bristol RE purchased new, heads into town along Marsh House Lane operating service 14 from Birchwood to the Bus Station in July 1981. The railway bridge in the background carries sidings into Rylands Coronation Wire Works and Central Station goods yard, with a second bridge beyond carrying the main line through Warrington Central.

The location is relatively unchanged in April 2015 although the premises of electrical wholesalers Taylor Trading have been demolished, the land becoming a car park. Optare Versa 98 (YJ13 HKE), one of six new in 2013 and route-branded for the Connect 17 services introduced that year, passes on a 17C working to Callands. Historically, many of Warrington's services were cross-town but these are now the only ones remaining.

In July 2014 the view is not that different as Volvo B7RLE/Wrightbus 93 (DK09 EMX) heads into town on service 23 from Cinnamon Brow. Trees have grown up on the disused railway sidings and an advertising hoarding appears next to the railway bridge whilst subtle changes to the houses in respect of their chimneys, roofs and windows can be discerned.

Turning from Lovely Lane into the Sankey Green roundabout operating service 14 from Dallam to Birchwood in November 1981 is East Lancs-bodied Leyland Atlantean 26 (OTB 26W), one of a batch of five new earlier that year which were the last Atlanteans purchased new before Warrington's buying policy changed to Dennis Dominators and Leyland Olympians. The imposing Co-op building dominates the scene advertising, amongst other things, a can of soup for 7½p!

Westy is an area of Latchford comprising mainly inter-war council housing, some of which is visible in this view of former London Transport DMS Daimler Fleetline/Metro-Cammell 98 (THM 503M) at the Kingsway Co-op bus stop in Richmond Avenue in August 1985 operating cross-town service 1A from Westy (Nook Lane) to Orford (Cleveland Road). This was one of six DMSs acquired from dealer Ensign in 1980, who converted them to single-doorway. The London Transport destination indicators were changed by Warrington to its standard layout before the buses entered service.

The location was essentially unchanged when photographed in April 2015. Now known as Westy Late Shop, the bus shelter has gone. Fairbrother F27 (V183 MEV), a formerly dual-doorway Alexander ALX400-bodied Dennis Trident new to East London operates the Westy Circular 1C returning to the Interchange.

Family-run Warrington operator Fairbrother runs three services marketed as '£1 To Town' (although the fare is now £1.30); the 1C Westy Circular, 16X to Dallam and the 21X Orford Circular. Still in London red and retaining its dual-doorway, Fairbrother's F36 (LJ03 MKV), an Alexander ALX400-bodied DAF DB250 new to Arriva London North, heads for the Interchange on a 16X journey in April 2015. The scene hasn't changed significantly although the busy roundabout is now traffic light-controlled. The Co-operative, as it is now branded, has lost its upper floor windows and ornate roof vents, to the detriment of its appearance.

LEFT: **East Lancs-bodied Daimler Fleetline 35 (NED 355M), one of six new in 1973, heads along Bradshaw Lane, Grappenhall, returning to town from Thelwall (with the blind not re-set) in April 1986. It is passing beneath the Warrington to Stockport railway which had closed to all traffic between Warrington and Skelton Junction (Timperley) the previous July. Before the construction of the Manchester Ship Canal the line had crossed Bradshaw Lane on the level and part of the old level-crossing keepers house, which became a private residence, is visible on the left. The building of the canal, which opened on 1 January 1894, required five railway lines which intersected its course to be diverted onto new parallel alignments in order to cross the canal on high-level girder bridges providing 75ft clearance above water level. Spoil excavated from the canal was used to construct long embankments up to these viaducts.**

RIGHT: **Apart from significant tree growth on the old railway trackbed the view was little-changed in April 2015 as DAF SB120/Wrightbus 55 (DK55 OMP) headed towards Warrington operating service 5 from Altrincham to the Interchange. The Latchford high-level bridge, about 600 yards to the left of this viewpoint, is still intact but sealed off; Railtrack planned to demolish it in 1997 but the Manchester Ship Canal company wouldn't agree to a request for a nine-day closure of the canal.**

Upon the break-up of North Western Road Car in March 1972, Warrington Corporation took on the operation of the four Warrington to Northwich services (43-46) jointly with Crosville, although they did not see regular double-deck operation until January 1985, when overhanging trees on the routes were lopped. East Lancs-bodied Daimler Fleetline 32 (NED 352M), new in 1973 as 101, heads north along the A49 in October 1985, crossing Acton swing bridge over the Weaver Navigation, on a Warrington-bound 44. A symmetrical bowstring girder bridge built in situ on an island in the centre of the river between 1931 and 1933, it was designed by J. A. Saner who was the Navigation's engineer. The brick building on the right is the bridge's control tower.

Warrington Borough Transport now only operates services 45 and 46 between Warrington and Northwich, and the only local bus service passing this location is the Saturdays-only X22 from Winsford to Liverpool which comprises one return journey operated by GHA Coaches, Ruabon. The 09.25 outward service from Winsford is depicted in April 2015 operated by W465 WGH, a Plaxton President-bodied Volvo B7TL new to London General in 2000. Changes are relatively few, although there are differences in the street lamps and the bus stop and shelter have gone.

Although a short section of the A57 Manchester Road in Woolston was re-aligned to give a straighter course, buses heading towards Warrington continued to use the old road. 84 (3712 ED), an East Lancs-bodied Leyland Titan PD2/40 new in 1962, was one of the last rear-entrance buses left in the fleet when photographed there in February 1980 operating cross-town service 79 from Woolston (Runnymede) to Longford (Chiltern Road), which was the last stamping ground of Warrington's Leyland Titans.

In August 2014 DAF SB120/Wrightbus 81 (YJ57 BRX) heads for Warrington Interchange. The saplings on the left in the previous picture have grown into mature trees over the intervening 34 years whilst the bus stop has been moved a few yards closer to the photographer and a shelter is now provided. The house in the background, with the electricity pylon beyond it, has had the pitched roof extended over the previously flat roof extension. The 79 has been replaced by the 3, which is extended just under a mile to Martinscroft (near the A57/M6 junction) and is no longer a cross-town service, the inner terminus now being at the Interchange.

Sometimes lucky, sometimes not

Tim Carter started taking bus photographs in 1986. He looks back at 30 years of lucky finds and occasional disappointments.

All photographs by the author

F rom my earliest memories, I have been interested in buses and coaches. Maybe it was in my blood. Two uncles worked at Plaxton and a couple of distant relatives drove for United Automobile Services.

Living in a village north of Scarborough on the A171, I can well remember on summer Saturdays watching what appeared to be a continuous line of buses and coaches travelling through Burniston on their way to the holiday resorts of Scarborough, Filey, Bridlington, as well as to Butlin's Filey Camp and the other numerous camping and holiday sites to be found south of Scarborough. These vehicles included examples from the fleets of United, Northern and its subsidiaries, the Scottish Bus Group, Venture and many other independents. The busiest period was

A lucky sighting in Scotland, the Strathclyde PTE Dodge with demountable Marshall bus body which was being operated by Arran Transport.

during the last two hours of the morning and into the afternoon. During the afternoon many of these buses and coaches could be seen returning north, taking home the previous week's holiday makers.

Though the A171 was nearly half a mile from our living room window, I could see United's vehicles on the 114 service between Scarborough, Cloughton and Ravenscar. The normal vehicles on this route were lowbridge Bristol Ks. United's Scarborough to Harwood Dale service passed even closer to our windows, and I can remember Bristol Ls operating this route. Being used to riding on a K when travelling into Scarborough with my mother, I was fascinated when the local press reported the arrival in Scarborough of the first Lodekka to be allocated to United's depot. It stated that once you were on the platform there were no more steps to climb. How were you to get to the top deck? Was there a lift? It certainly sounded like a giant leap forward from the Ks. I was only about five at the time and it was with a disappointment to see the actual vehicle complete with its stairs.

I also remember my first sighting of a Bristol RE while I was cycling between Burniston and Cloughton on the A171. At the time, United's Scarborough allocation of single deckers consisted of Bristol Ls, LSs and MWs, so to see an early RELL with the vertical wraparound windscreen heading towards me was certainly a startling sight. I was yet to discover *Buses Illustrated*, so had received no advance warning of the arrival of such a modern-looking vehicle.

My interest in buses and coaches continued through my teens. While I was undergoing teacher training at Loughborough between 1969 and 1972, a group of us decided to visit the Earl's Court Commercial Motor Show. I remember being more interested in the bus and coach section. How much was down to my latent interest and how much to the fact it was less crowded and I could actually see the exhibits and even go on board some of them, I'm not sure. At the same show I discovered *Buses* magazine, and upon my return to Loughborough, a regular order was placed and I continue to look forward to the delivery of the latest edition each month.

My interest continued during the next 15 years and occasionally I would take a photograph, but all was to change in my 36th year, 1986. Maybe it was all the talk of deregulation, but I started taking many more photos, a hobby which continues today.

The deeper interest may also be partly down to seeing my first material in print, which turned out to be an article rather than photograph.

In July 1987 a Northumbria MCW Metroliner was caught posed for publicity shots in Newcastle with driver and hostess smiling for the camera.

The Strathclyde PTE converted eight Alexander-bodied Atlanteans to 31-seat single-deckers in the 1980s. Sighting one of these was some compensation for the general lack of buses on Scotland's streets caused by a widespread strike at the Scottish Bus Group.

A stop at Watford Gap service area on the M1 motorway produced this lucky find, a new Bexleybus Olympian on delivery. It had a Northern Counties body.

A Stagecoach United Counties AEC Routemaster in Bedford Bus Station in January 1988 prior to the launch of Routemasters on a local service the following month.

Just over 25 years later another chance sighting in Bedford, with Stagecoach East displaying a new Volvo B11R ahead of the introduction of a fleet of new coaches to the X5 service linking Oxford and Cambridge in January 2015.

Throughout my 30 years of 'serious' bus photography I cannot recall a single expedition when the sole aim has been to capture an individual vehicle on film. There have been a variety of reasons for my trips, such as to record the bus scene in a specific area, to capture some of a new batch of vehicles in service, to see if any new vehicles can be seen on the first day of a new registration, or simply to see what was out and about. Some trips have resulted in some lucky sightings, while others have been disappointing..

A trip to north-east England and Scotland in the summer of 1987 provided the full gambit of emotions; some lucky sightings and some disappointments. One day needed some careful planning, as I wanted to visit Lindisfarne Castle on Holy Island. Access is via a causeway, which is impassable at high tide. Knowing that Northumbria's Berwick-upon-Tweed to Holy Island service was variable, depending on the state of the tide, a stamped addressed envelope was sent for a timetable. With that information a visit was planned and hopefully a photograph could be taken of the bus on the causeway. Waiting at the mainland end of the causeway allowed me to photograph a VRT in Northumbria's new livery speeding across the causeway.

During that holiday there were several lucky sightings. While in Newcastle and passing Northumbria's former United depot in Gallowgate, Metroliner 160 (C160 UHN) was standing on the forecourt being photographed in the newly applied grey based livery. Later in that holiday two rare vehicles were captured on film. In Glasgow, I saw Strathclyde's SA5 (KSU 855P) one of the Alexander-bodied Leyland Atlanteans which had been converted from double-deckers in 1983-84. The second also carried Strathclyde Transport livery, it being Arran Transport B949 YHS, a Dodge which had demountable bus and truck bodies.

It was while in Scotland that a disappointment was experienced. Scottish Bus Group crews were in dispute with company management. For part of our holiday all Central, Clydeside and Kelvin vehicles were withdrawn from service, while Highland, Lowland and Northern were partly withdrawn. While some buses were recorded in service, many were parked up in depots and bus stations. There was the consolation of Lothian, Strathclyde and Grampian vehicles being available to photograph in service.

Over the years there have been several incidents of being in the right place at the right time. In August 1987, a stop was made at Watford Gap service area on the M1 motorway and standing in the southbound parking area was an unregistered Northern Counties-bodied Leyland Olympian in the new cream and blue Bexleybus livery for Selkent service in the Bexley area. This vehicle was to full Great Manchester specification and the route number blind was set to 001, so maybe it was the first of the batch.

A year and a half later, a visit to London included a look at what was operating in the Victoria area. While there, MXX 367, a Guy Special/ECW came into view. This maroon, former London Transport GS-class vehicle was operating a special service to the IMREX 89 Model Exhibition. I had never seen a GS in operation before.

Twice I have had lucky sightings from the same point in Bedford. One Saturday morning in January 1988, I glanced down Harpur Street toward the Town Hall and caught a glimpse of a Routemaster in United Counties post privatisation green livery. A quick dash to the bus station and I was able to photograph it parking up in the lay-over area. At this stage it carried

no branding and was presumably on driver training before a batch of Routemasters was introduced on the cross town 101 route in February.

Eighteen years later, while in Bedford collecting a few last minute items before going on holiday, I again glanced down the now pedestrianised Harpur Street. Standing there was a tri-axle Plaxton Elite in two-tone blue livery. Closer inspection revealed it to be one of the new Stagecoach Volvo B11Rs for the X5 Oxford to Cambridge service. Staff were on hand to publicise the new vehicles which were due to be introduced a few weeks later on 4 January 2015.

Even while on holiday abroad, I am on the lookout for buses and coaches worth photographing. The variety in Malta (pre-Arriva) and Madeira being just two examples. During the spring of 2014, a trip on the Hurtigruten cruise line's MS Polarlys for its coastal voyage provided the opportunity to photograph many buses and coaches and some unusual sights – certainly to British eyes. Late one afternoon in a northern town, I saw a driver attaching snow chains to the rear wheels, before he took his vehicle out for an evening run. At another port of call, I caught sight of what appeared to be a vehicle with part bus body, part goods vehicle. We were in port long enough for me to go ashore and take a closer look to find it was a Volvo in the Boreal Transport fleet with standard coach bodywork for the front half and a box van body

Spotted from a cruise ship in Norway, a Boreal Transport Volvo 9700S with a combined bus/van body.

This Post Office mobile exhibition bus conveniently came to the author, with a visit to the school where he was teaching. It is a former London Transport Daimler Fleetline.

How many buses have a registration number that coincides with their seating capacity? Stagecoach 14000 (F110 NES) is a 110-seat Alexander-bodied Leyland Olympian.

Double-deckers cut down to single-deckers are rare. This former Ribble Bristol VRT is seen in service with Guide Friday. It spent two seasons, 1998-99, on the Cotswold Tour.

for the rear half. It brought back memories of the Arran Transport Dodge seen on the Isle of Arran in 1987 and of MacBraynes buses seen on childhood visits to Scotland. Although these had complete bus bodywork, many had a goods compartment towards the rear.

These are just a few of the lucky sightings I have made during my 30 years of bus photography. Others have included Guide Friday CBV 9S, a former Ribble Bristol VRT/ECW double-decker which was converted by Guide Friday into a single-decker. This vehicle was captured on film during a very brief visit to Stratford-upon-Avon in September 1998.

One final lucky sighting was during a visit to London Luton Airport. While travelling to the airport, I spotted a tri-axle Mercedes-Benz Citaro outside a hotel. This left-hand-drive vehicle was parked up between visits to FirstGroup subsidiaries when Mercedes was trying to raise interest in its 15m-long bus.

Sometimes a bus or former bus might even come to me. In April 1987, a mobile exhibition unit for the Post Office was due to visit the school where I was teaching. It turned out to be an ex-London Transport DMS, complete with a generator trailer. It was parked outside my workshop for its visit. The opportunity to take a few photographs could not be missed.

Another example of what might be referred to as a vehicle coming to me, is also maybe the closest I have come to a trip out in the hope of capturing a specific vehicle – even if it was by proxy. Early in 1989, Stagecoach announced that it was taking delivery of three 12m Leyland Olympians with Alexander RL bodies. Shortly afterwards my parents were visiting and a planned shopping trip to Northampton would take them past the United counties depot in Bedford Road. They were asked to keep an eye open outside the depot, and take a picture if a tri-axle double-decker was seen. They of course had no success as *Buses* later recorded that two with 96 coach seats had gone to Cumberland, and F110 NES with 110 bus seats was with Stagecoach's Magicbus operation in Glasgow. After only a short time in Glasgow it was transferred to East Midlands. Little did I realise that later it would be transferred to my local depot, specifically for the 07.35 Biggleswade to Bedford service. This timing had often required two buses because of the heavy loading; F110 NES could cope with the demand on its own. It has now been repainted in its original livery, complete with Megadekka branding and is still to be seen regularly performing a school run in Bedford. ∎

ENVIRO⁴⁰⁰:
The First Decade

The ADL Enviro400 is Britain's most popular double-decker.
Mark Bailey illustrates a selection.

The Stagecoach group has by far the largest fleet of Enviro400s, with the first integral examples entering service in 2006. East Midland 19132 was one of a pair operated for Nottinghamshire County Council on Lynx services connecting Retford and Worksop with Robin Hood Airport near Doncaster. It was photographed in June 2008 arriving in Retford on route 29 from the airport.

It was in 2005 that Alexander Dennis (ADL) introduced the Enviro400 double-decker, and since then it has become a familiar sight across the length and breadth of the country. The vast majority are of integrated construction based on an updated version of the Dennis Trident chassis, but significant numbers have also been built on the Scania N230UD, primarily for the Stagecoach group. A small number were built on Volvo B9TL chassis for Dublin Bus, East Yorkshire and London General, a solitary Volvo B7TL was bodied in 2006 and is operated by Bluestar, and in 2015 Stagecoach received B5LHs with Enviro400 bodies.

The drive towards cleaner, greener transport has seen a growing number of Enviro400s enter service utilising hybrid technology, particularly in London. In 2012 the ADL chassis was coded E40D for diesels and E40H for hybrids, although the complete bus is still marketed as the Enviro400 or Enviro400H respectively.

Despite being the UK's best selling double-decker, in 2014 ADL announced a redesign of the Enviro400 as part of its Major Model Change (MMC) programme – a move designed to protect the company's market-leading position. This included a complete overhaul of construction to improve build quality, the use of Euro6 low-emission engines as standard, and a restyled appearance. ∎

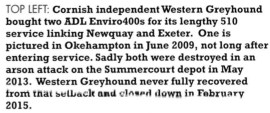

TOP LEFT: Cornish independent Western Greyhound bought two ADL Enviro400s for its lengthy 510 service linking Newquay and Exeter. One is pictured in Okehampton in June 2009, not long after entering service. Sadly both were destroyed in an arson attack on the Summercourt depot in May 2013. Western Greyhound never fully recovered from that setback and closed down in February 2015.

UPPER MIDDLE: In January 2006 the first production examples of the Enviro400 entered service with Metroline in London, on route 24 from Pimlico to Hampstead Heath. TE890 (LK08 NVE) is from a later batch, pictured at Marble Arch in May 2010 working the 16 from Cricklewood to Victoria. Unfortunate Transport for London regulations have since forced the removal of the attractive blue relief from Metroline buses operating TfL services.

LOWER MIDDLE: In late 2009 Stagecoach Devon took delivery of 13 new vehicles in a major investment for the increasingly popular Exeter park-and-ride services. Included in the mix were three ADL Enviro400s in a red and yellow livery for the Honiton Road Red route. 19570 (WA59 FWS) is seen approaching the park-and-ride site in March 2010.

BOTTOM: Built as a demonstrator in 2006, SN56 AWX is unique, being the only Enviro400 on a Volvo B7TL chassis. In 2007 it was acquired by Go-Ahead subsidiary Solent Blue Line and is pictured in Eastleigh bus station in October 2009 on Bluestar service 2 from Southampton to Fair Oak.

TOP RIGHT: JP Travel of Middleton bought a new Enviro400 in 2009 after having a demonstrator on loan from ADL. Numbered 551, named Charlotte, and with personalised registration VT59 JPT, it is seen here in April 2011 leaving Middleton bus station on service 156 from Manchester to Langley. It was sold to Ensignbus in 2012 and on again to First Essex the following year. JP Travel was acquired by Stagecoach Manchester in 2014.

BOTTOM RIGHT: As well as operating integral E400s, the Stagecoach group is the largest customer for the Enviro400 body on the Scania N230UD chassis, with over 500 in service. Representative of the type is 15672 (KX10 KTA) of Midland Red South, seen in April 2011 arriving in Evesham on route 28 from Stratford-upon-Avon.

ABOVE: In a surprise move in 2011 Connex Jersey acquired two ADL Enviro400 demonstrators, reintroducing double-deck operation to the island after a gap of 40 years. They were used on route 15 linking the airport with St. Helier, and 1184 (J 57156), formerly SN60 CAA, is pictured during its first week in service in June 2011 in St. Aubin. Both were sold in 2013 and this one is now with First Eastern Counties.

TOP LEFT: Essex-based Ensignbus has bought and sold a number of Enviro400s in its dealer capacity, and a few have also entered its operational fleet, if only for a short time. One is former demonstrator SN59 AWV, numbered 123 by Ensignbus and subsequently sold on to First Essex. It is pictured in January 2012 arriving at the Lakeside shopping centre on service 83 from Chadwell St. Mary, with its destination already set for a return on the 73 to Grays and Tilbury.

BOTTOM LEFT: In 2007 East Yorkshire took delivery of five Enviro400s on Volvo B9TL chassis, one of only a handful of operators to take that combination. Four years later it introduced ten hybrid Enviro400H integrals and seized the opportunity to boldly promote the benefits of the greener technology on all four sides of the vehicles. One is seen in Hull city centre in August 2011 working route 57 from Hessle to Longhill.

TOP RIGHT: **The number of First group's hybrid Enviro400Hs was more than halved in 2013 when its London operations were sold to Tower Transit, leaving ten with First Glasgow and eight with First Somerset & Avon. Illustrating the latter is 39140 (SN62 AXB), seen at the Odd Down park-and-ride facility in June 2013 working route 41 into Bath city centre in conjunction with Bath and North East Somerset Council.**

BOTTOM RIGHT: **The National Express group operates several hundred Enviro400s across the West Midlands and Tayside. In 2013 nine hybrid versions entered service in Dundee sporting the green and white livery used by the group to promote its low-emission fleet. Pictured in the city centre in August 2013 is 5430 (SP13 BTE), working cross-city service 5 from Ninewells Hospital to the Barnhill district of Broughty Ferry.**

BELOW: **Suffolk independent Carters bought a new ADL Enviro400 in 2008 where it remained the only example in the fleet. Numbered 458 (AY58 CYJ), it was photographed in January 2012 turning into the Old Cattle Market bus station in Ipswich on service 92 from Cattawade. It was sold in 2013 to Travelmasters of Sheerness.**

ABOVE: **The only Enviro400s in the fleet of Lothian Buses are 15 hybrid variants delivered in 2011. Representative of the batch is 206 (SN61 BBJ), photographed in Edinburgh's Princes Street in August 2013 on service 10 from Torphin to Western Harbour.**

BELOW: **Go-Ahead subsidiary Plymouth Citybus operates 20 ADL Enviro400s, with a further ten due in 2015. Four are liveried and branded for the Blue Flash service launched in 2013 to compete with First Devon & Cornwall on the Tavistock corridor. 502 (WF63 LZB) is seen at Yelverton in November 2013 on its way back to Plymouth on route 12.**

ABOVE: **The Dutch-owned Abellio group acquired its London operations from National Express in 2009 and has a sizeable fleet of both diesel and hybrid Enviro400s. Pictured at Hyde Park Corner in March 2014 is diesel example 9535 (SN12 ACF), working route C2 from Parliament Hill Fields to Victoria.**

BELOW: **North Wales independent Express Motors operates two Enviro400-bodied Scania N280UDs, the only examples of this combination. The first of the pair is CY12 EMS, seen in Llanberis in August 2014 returning to Caernarfon on the 88, a route picked up when Padarn Bus went into liquidation a few months earlier.**

ABOVE: One of the first operators to take delivery of the new MMC Enviro400s was Reading Buses, with a batch of eight diesel examples to add to 31 hybrid Enviro400Hs already in service. Branded for claret routes and working the 21 to Lower Earley, one is pictured outside Reading station when new in October 2014.

BELOW: In 2013 Arriva introduced its Sapphire premium brand on selected routes, with smart uniformed drivers and higher specification vehicles in an attractive new livery. Sapphire coverage has since been extended to further routes, including Arriva Cymru 12 from Llandudno to Rhyl. Newly-delivered Enviro400 4553 (CX14 AZL) is pictured in August 2014 under a brooding sky waiting time at Llandudno's West Shore.

Growing up in black and white

Remember roll film? **Gavin Booth** goes back to the days of black-and-white negatives.

All photographs by the author

Possibly the author's first-ever bus photo – the print reflects his lack of proper care when handling negatives. It is one of Edinburgh Corporation's 300 Leyland Titan PD2/20s with Metro-Cammell Orion bodies, brand-new at the Braids terminus in August 1956, in the final months of the Edinburgh trams. On the same spool are photos of trams at the same spot taken on the same day.

My grandchildren look at me pityingly when I talk of a world without television, computers, iPads, Wiis and XBoxes, and when they talk about PS1s they mean the games console rather that the early postwar Leyland Tiger. Even my children raise their eyes heavenward when I tell them how lucky they are to have all this technology at their fingertips, when I had to make do with steam radio, a typewriter, board games, a Dansette record player and a Box Brownie camera.

Don't get me wrong. I am more than happy with my digital cameras, their quality, ease of use and almost limitless memories – but I still look back with affection at growing up between the 1940s and the

Life then – we know from Pathé and Gaumont-British newsreels at the cinema – was in black and white and although it has become a cliché, that really is how I remember it. The postwar austerity years could be as grim as they are often depicted, with ration books, no TV in the Booth household until the late 1950s, drab clothing and black cars. All British-built, of course. Even my school uniform – something we seemed to wear most of the time we were not in pyjamas – observed the school colours of black, white and grey.

It was the Coronation in 1953 that prompted Britain to start bursting into colour and optimism. I marked the New Elizabethan age by spending every spare moment spotting railway locomotives

Elizabethan was just that – the eponymous train, the most glamorous one of the day, linking Edinburgh Waverley and London Kings Cross stations in just six-and-a-half hours, non-stop, and always headed by a pristine streamlined A4 Pacific. But when I realised that I had 'copped' every locomotive likely to work into Edinburgh, I found myself drawn to trams and buses. And there I've stayed ever since.

Photography wasn't as easy or cheap as it is now, so I didn't photograph all the things I now wish that I had. My father's Box Brownie was the simplest of cameras, virtually a completely non-adjustable pinhole box with a lens, that accommodated an eight-exposure Kodak 120-size black-and-white spool that

ABOVE: **Although most of my early attempts at bus photography were of static vehicles because of the limitations of the Box Brownie, with the Retinette I became more adventurous and tried moving shots. I have always liked this one, taken in 1965 on Edinburgh's High Street and featuring one of Edinburgh Corporation's 100 Weymann-bodied Leyland Tiger Cubs bought in 1959-61 to replace a fleet of elderly single-deckers, some dating back to the mid-1930s. While the buildings in the background have not changed in the past 50 years, business names have: the National Commercial Bank of Scotland – itself a 1959 merger of the separate National and Commercial banks – was merged with the Royal Bank of Scotland in 1959; Patrick Thomson was a big department store. The Midlothian-registered 1938 Rover was still used as everyday transport. This Tiger Cub was sold, with 47 others, to the Ulster Transport Authority in 1966 when removal of low bridges and road-lowering rendered them surplus to Edinburgh's requirements.**

LEFT: **This is the sort of situation where the faster Kodak Tri-X film came into its own – a wintry scene at Elm Row, Edinburgh, with one of the 72 Birmingham-style Metro-Cammell-bodied Daimlers bought by Edinburgh Corporation in 1949/50 to reinforce the postwar fleet. All but 10 were CVG6 models with Gardner 6LW engines, and the others, like 113 here, were CVD6s with Daimler CD6 engines; for local enthusiasts, the larger headlamps of the CVD6s made for easy recognition. These Daimlers were the backbone of the double-deck fleet until the mid-1950s and were withdrawn between 1962 and 1967; the CVD6s were the first to go.**

The Retinette camera encouraged a bit of experimentation, hence this shot of a 1955 Edinburgh Corporation Leyland Titan, sun-dappled among the trees that line the road through The Meadows in Edinburgh in 1965. There were, famously, 300 of these lightweight buses delivered between 1954 and 1957 to complete the replacement of Edinburgh's first-generation electric trams, and some survived in service until 1976, although the bus here, 596, was withdrawn in 1973 after a decent 18 years service. It's one of these photos I wish now I had taken in colour, but colour photography was pretty expensive, and I held out with black-and-white into the early 1970s.

Growing up in a city with two large principal bus operators, it was fascinating to read of independents and intriguing to learn of the co-operatives in Ayrshire, where several operators combined to provide services using a common fleetname. This is the AA bus station in Ayr in 1958 with a service ready to depart for Stewarton. Although labelled AA Motor Services Ltd, it is a bus from the fleet of Dodds of Troon – the 'DT No5' fleetnumber is a clue. Dodds had a major involvement in AA (the initials stood for Ayr-Ardrossan, the core route), and favoured Gardner-engined Guys; the other AA members favoured Daimlers (Tumilty) or Leylands (Young). This bus started life in 1943 as a Glasgow Corporation Guy Arab II double-decker and after sale in 1951 passed to Dodds who had the chassis lengthened and this 30ft-long Darlington Corporation-style Roe 38-seat centre entrance body fitted.

had to be loaded and unloaded in darkness to avoid light spoiling the film. You pointed the camera, held it steady and pressed the shutter release, remembering to wind it on one place each time in case you found yourself with interesting but useless double-exposures.

With only eight exposures under your control, you had to choose your subjects wisely. Then when your spool was finished, you carefully extracted it and handed it into your local chemist and waited for several days before you could collect a set of prints, usually the small (63mm x 90mm) contact-size prints that were all my pocket money would allow. No chance to review your photos immediately, or to delete the duffers.

And if you wanted to see them in print in *Buses Illustrated* – and I did – then you had the extra expense of a postcard-size print from the negative, again via the chemists.

The Box Brownie was essentially a fair weather camera, but my discovery of 400ASA Kodak Tri-X film allowed photography to become an all-year activity. And as pocket money increased and the family horizons expanded – Scarborough, Blackpool, Norfolk, London and the south coast – so my photo collection increased.

The 1960s equivalent of a selfie – the author, Retinette in hand, capturing himself and a BEA Routemaster in his shot. The 65 short forward-entrance Routemasters operated by London Transport for British European Airways towed luggage trailers on their frequent journeys between the air terminal in London's Cromwell Road and Heathrow Airport, a considerably smaller place in the mid-1960s than it is today, and where today photography like this is likely to be regarded with some suspicion. These were the only short-length forward entrance Routemasters built.

The Brownie camera was certainly simple, but the big 120-size negatives – black-and-white of course – sometimes led to very acceptable images.

Trouble is, the Box Brownie didn't look cool, and I aspired to cameras that looked more grown-up, even when their results were little better than those from the Brownie. Only a venture into 35mm film with a Kodak Retinette camera and the natural progression to a long line of Canon SLRs moved me into more serious photography.

Today I have a digital Canon EOS and – sorry about this, Canon – a Nikon Coolpix P7100 and love them both, though I find myself copping out and using the wee Nikon for most expeditions and the Canon only comes out for special occasions, such is the quality of the smaller and lighter camera. OK, I'm getting old.

My family and friends rebuke me when I head off for a day chasing bus photos, suggesting that I must have photos of all these buses already, so why bother? Maybe I have, but that's not the point is it – support me on this, *Buses Yearbook* readers. There is the immense pleasure of getting the photo you wanted and I'm sure it was the same half a century ago with the early black-and-whites you'll see in this selection. Technically they are sometimes a bit dodgy, but to a teenager that didn't really matter. ■

ABOVE RIGHT: **Laurie of Hamilton, trading as Chieftain, ran services into the expanding new town of East Kilbride, until the business was acquired by Scottish Bus Group's Central SMT company in 1961. This former London Transport Leyland Titan/Park Royal RTL was new in 1953 and passed to Chieftain after just six years in London service; Scottish independents always recognised a bargain. It is seen at the company's Burnbank garage in 1959, newly repainted before going into Chieftain service. It passed to Central SMT with 30 other buses, ranging from a prewar Birmingham Leyland to two recently bought Leyland Atlanteans. Chieftain 47 (NLE 738) stayed with Central until 1966.**

RIGHT: **Renfrew Ferry bus terminus was always a busy place in the 1950s and 1960s, with services from Paisley provided jointly by two independents, Cunningham and Paton, with other services operated by McGill's and Western SMT. On a wet day in 1965, its conductress makes her way to LSN 286, a 1960 Daimler CSG6-30 with Northern Counties body. It had been new to Garelochhead Coach Services, passing to Cunningham and later to Longstaff, Mirfield. The CSG6-30 had a David Brown synchromesh gearbox rather than the pre-select or semi-automatic gearboxes fitted to most Daimlers since the 1930s.**

BELOW: **Lincoln was a stop-over on the way home from family holidays in Norfolk, and on a wet day in the mid-1960s, Lincoln Corporation 97, a 1964 Leyland Atlantean PDR1/1 with Roe body, picks up outside the railway station.**

LEFT: **Carlisle was reasonably accessible from Edinburgh, and this 1954 United Bristol KSW6B with 60-seat ECW body is seen on a Carlisle local service. Although United Automobile Services was normally associated with north-east England, it had an outpost in Ribble territory in Carlisle until early 1969, when the newly-formed National Bus Company transferred this operation to Ribble along with 24 vehicles, mostly single-deckers. In the days before NBC was created, United had been a Tilling Group company, and Ribble had been part of the BET Group. This photo is likely to have been taken on 11 August 1968 when the author visited Carlisle to witness the 'Fifteen-guinea special', the last steam-hauled main line passenger train on British Railways – at least until preserved locomotives were allowed back. Fifteen guineas was £15 15s – or £15.75 in decimal currency. Vaux, the brewery advertising on the front of the bus, and John Collier, the tailor's shop on the right, were once familiar names, now long vanished.**

LEFT: **Winter 1970 in a snowbound Paris and there are still takers for the upper deck of this intriguing Saviem sightseeing bus.**

One of the more unusual coaches to emerge from the Scottish Omnibuses New Street depot in Edinburgh was this Continental Trailways Bus & Car Eagle – Belgian-built – in Scotland on a Visit the USA tourist mission in the early 1960s. The Eagle range was produced by various builders for Continental Trailways as a rival to Greyhound's Scenicruiser.

This was the sad and rather scary end of Scottish Omnibuses B387, a 1949 AEC Regal III with Burlingham Seagull-style body. It was 4 July 1964 and with two other enthusiasts I had set off by car to photograph buses in the Scottish Borders. We set ourselves up for photos of the bus on the Duns to Abbey St. Bathans route – just two journeys on a Saturday – and once B387 had passed us we piled into the car to pursue it. When we caught it up this what we found – off the road resting against a tree that was preventing it from plunging hundreds of feet into the Blackadder Water below. No mobile phones then, so we phoned the police from a nearby house after we had checked that the driver and conductor were OK; there had been no passengers, fortuitously. We continued our journey once the police had arrived, but returned on the way home to see what was happening. By this time B387 was partially recovered, thanks to the joint effort of the Edinburgh tow-wagon and another Regal III. A few days later the battered B387 appeared in the withdrawn bay at Scottish Omnibuses' Edinburgh New Street depot.

RIGHT: **Acquisitions by the Scottish Bus Group companies kept enthusiasts busy in the 1960s. Scottish Omnibuses bought the popular independent, Baxter's of Airdrie, in 1962, bringing a varied fleet of buses into the fleet, including some that had been ordered before the take-over and were delivered new to Scottish Omnibuses. One was DD961, a 1963 Daimler Fleetline CRG6LX with the first example of the Alexander D-type lowheight body. It initially ran in the company's light green/off white, as seen leaving Buchanan Street bus station in Glasgow on the long 310 route to Edinburgh, but in 1964 was transferred to the Baxter's fleet, which was using that company's former blue livery for its local services. In 1965 the bus was burned out but was rebodied with a similar Alexander body.**

No Health & Safety concerns in the mid-1960s as Scottish Omnibuses crews on the 309 Edinburgh-Glasgow express service change over on the busy (and dangerous) three-lane A8 road linking the two cities. Both buses are Alexander Y type AEC Reliances from a substantial batch bought in 1964.

Middlesbrough Corporation operated some of the earliest Daimler Fleetlines. This is a 1962 example, when new, caught on the Box Brownie in the town centre. The neat Northern Counties body sat well on the Fleetline chassis.

Travel West Midlands 4001, a DAF DB250 with Optare Spectra body, was one of the first low-floor double-deckers to enter service in Britain, in February 1998. It is seen at the Merry Hill shopping centre in 2001.

The low-down on low floors

Paul Godding analyses the first generation of low-floor buses which joined the Travel West Midlands fleet between 1996 and 2000.

All photographs by the author.

Travel West Midlands, part of the National Express Group, was an early adopter of low-floor buses and one of the first operators to run a low-floor double-decker. Between 1996 and 2000 it bought almost 700 new accessible buses, with over half of them being supplied by Volvo.

Now, 20 years after the first Volvo B6LE entered service, some of these early low-floor models have gone from the fleet, while others are fast disappearing. Whether people like them or not, they have all served the West Midlands well and led a movement which has brought low-floor buses to every route.

VOLVO B6LE

The first large batch of low-floor buses for Travel West Midlands comprised 50 Volvo B6LEs with Wright Crusader bodies, and the company went on to build up the largest fleet of Wright-bodied B6LEs with a total of 183 in service at its peak. The vehicles had 37 seats, although the seating inside was quite sparse for the first quarter of the vehicle, with most of the seats beyond the centre bulkhead. The type has sometimes been seen as the poor man's Dennis Dart, but the B6LEs served many areas with a degree of reliability, and from an enthusiast perspective a bit of entertainment was guaranteed especially on the hilly routes around Dudley.

A small batch of B6LEs was also operated by Acocks Green, including a period on the short-lived service 38A linking the city with the airport, but they were never a common sight in Birmingham.

The first B6LE withdrawal took place in 2003 as a result of fire damage. The first routine withdrawals started in 2010 and by the end of the year quite a number had gone. Withdrawals continued unabated for the next 18 months, but from late 2013 the fleet stabilised at around 30 vehicles.

In 2015 just 15 of the type remained in service at Wolverhampton, which was an odd choice for the type as this garage had only briefly operated B6LEs at the start of the millenium, with a gap of ten years before the next substantial allocation.

VOLVO B10L DIESEL

Travel West Midlands had two types of B10Ls on its books, 80 Wright Liberator-bodied examples and 14 with Alexander Ultra bodies. All were delivered in 1997 and were the company's first full-size low-floor buses. TWM was the biggest UK user of the B10L.

The majority of the Wright-bodied B10Ls were in TWM livery from new, although the last seven came in the colours of Smiths, with Travel Your Bus fleetnames. This business had been taken over by TWM in 1993.

Most of the 80 Liberators were fitted with Voith gearboxes but, as was common with TWM at the time, a few had ZF gearboxes. Where the mid-sized B6LE used Volvo's 5.48-litre D6A engine, the 12m-long B10L used the more familiar 9.6-litre DH10A.

Many of the B10Ls went into service on some of TWM's busiest routes with Superline branding, others took over Hagley Road services as well as

Dudley, Walsall and West Bromwich were their key operating areas, with them serving places around the Black Country, such as Stourbridge, Merry Hill and Halesowen, but also operating as far east as Sutton Coldfield, Burntwood and even Cannock on occasion. Dudley and Merry Hill in particular were hubs for the type.

Travel West Midlands started introducing low-floor buses to its fleet in 1996. First-generation buses delivered new were:

Manufacturer	Quantity	Fleet numbers	Delivered
Volvo B6LE/Wright Crusader	183	501-683	1996-99
Scania L113/Wright Access Ultralow	2	1398-1399	1996
Volvo B10L/Wright Liberator	80	1401-80	1997
Volvo B10L/Alexander Ultra CNG	14	1501-14	1997
Scania L94/Wright Access Floline	1	1400	1998
Mercedes-Benz O405N	193	1515-1707	1998-99
Mercedes-Benz O405GN artic	11	6001-6011	1999
Optare Spectra	22	4001-4022	1998-99
Optare Solo	45	276-320	1999
Optare Excel	35	684-718	1999
Volvo B7TL/Plaxton President	102	4023-4124	1999-2000

Externally, there's little to distinguish the Volvo B7L with Wright body from the more common B10BLE. The B7L has a full-length low floor, and on the B7L the body is known as the Liberator. Line 33 branding is carried by this bus in central Birmingham in 2002.

operations from Travel Your Bus. However some B10L-operated routes, including the Hagley Road services, soon lost their B10Ls in favour of double-deckers to provide increased capacity. This allowed B10Ls to take over other routes, replacing step-entrance Leyland Lynxes and Volvo B10Bs.

The B10Ls could be found at many TWM garages. The transfer of B10Ls to Wolverhampton in 2010 marked a milestone for the company, as they ousted the final step-entrance buses from the fleet, making it 100 per cent low-floor. For a short time the B10Ls worked local services around the town. However the delivery of new Scania OmniLinks saw the Wolverhampton B10Ls being replaced by T- and R-registered Mercedes, with the B10Ls moving to

Unusual vehicles in the TWM fleet were 14 B10Ls which had CNG engines and Alexander Ultra bodies. They were based in Walsall.

Perry Bar. Routine withdrawals started in 2011; the last of the B10Ls survive in Walsall.

VOLVO B10L CNG

The 14 CNG-powered B10Ls with Alexander Belfast Ultra bodies were allocated from new to Walsall and were branded for service 529. These buses also carried British Gas branding to promote the fact that they were being powered by compressed natural gas rather than diesel. The arrival of Dennis Tridents on the 529 in 2001 ousted the gas buses to secondary services around Walsall.

By 2007 a small number had been withdrawn from service and transferred to the training fleet, leaving the remaining examples in normal service around Walsall until 2010, by which time their gas bus identity was long gone and the CNG engines had been replaced by reconditioned diesel engines. Withdrawal for those still in regular service came in 2010, although nine were reinstated for passenger service at Yardley Wood for 18 months.

Three have so far been sold for scrap with a fourth being used as a non-PSV for trade union Unite; the remainder are either withdrawn, or active in the training fleet.

MERCEDES-BENZ O405N

Following the unusual (in the UK) B10Ls, by far the rarest low-floor type to enter service with Travel West Midlands were the 193 Mercedes Benz O405Ns in 1998-99. Although commonplace throughout the world, even today, they were rare in the UK and despite the previous step-entrance O405 being used by a greater number of individual operators, the low-floor fleet at TWM alone outnumbered all of the earlier step-entrance models in the UK..

The first eight of the O405s were completed in the UK by UVG, but with the closure of that business the rest of the vehicles were finished by Mercedes.

The early batch of R- and S-registered buses entered service on key routes across the West Midlands and Warwickshire. The allocations were spread between West Bromwich, Birmingham Central and Coventry. These were followed a year later by a further 79 examples which came with high-backed seating and were initially split between Hockley and Lea Hall.

The fleet stayed fairly static for many years, but 2007/08 would see the start of the changes for the type. With the arrival of large numbers of Scania OmniLinks there was some re-allocation of Mercs.

One was taken out of service in 2001 following extensive fire damage, and was replaced by an ex-demonstrator which was numbered 1743 to match its registration, S343 MOJ. The next withdrawal came in July 2010 when 1583 was withdrawn as life-expired, and this started a steady decline of the type.

LEFT: **The 11 Mercedes O405GN artics latterly operated in Coventry.**

BELOW: **The most numerous type among TWM's initial low-floor models was the Mercedes-Benz O405, of which there were 204, including 11 articulated versions. In this 2003 view in Coventry a five-year-old Mercedes carries distinctive PrimeLine branding which was used on high-quality routes operated in partnership with Centro and the city council.**

TWM also operated the only UK Mercedes-Benz O405GN artics. Eleven entered service at Perry Barr on route 67 complete with route branding, and remained on this service until 2004 when they were replaced by Scania OmniCity artics. The O405GNs then moved to Coventry, where they operated until 2011.

OPTARE SPECTRA

The first low-floor double-deckers for Travel West Midlands were 22 Optare Spectra-bodied DAF DB250s. The first, 4001 with registration R1 NEG (for National Express Group), was one of the first

Two of the pioneering low-floor Optare Spectras in Wolverhampton in 2010.

low-floor double-deckers in service when it took to the streets of Birmingham in February 1998. The bulk of the Spectras entered service at Birmingham Central in 1999 where they were allocated to route

50, branded as City Fifty. They stayed on the 50s until 2001 when Alexander-bodied Volvo B7TLs took over, and the Spectras were cascaded onto other routes. They remained in service at Birmingham Central until 2009 when the remaining 21 examples were transferred to Wolverhampton where they took over local routes previously operated by MCW Metrobuses.

The first withdrawal was 4014 which was as a result of an arson attack in 2001, the next to go was 4007 13 years later with 4003 following suit, a further reduction in the fleet took place during the early part of 2015.

OPTARE SOLO

TWM's 45 new Optare Solos were 27-seaters of the M850 variant and were delivered in 1999. Although most were in low-floor livery, a small number also carried route branding, including the Bushbury Mini and the Harborne Hopper, as well as the 500 which was the free shuttle bus from Wolverhampton bus station to the town centre.

Those bought new were later joined by further examples from Travel London and its successor, Connex Bus.

A number of Solos were transferred to sister operations in Dundee for use with Travel Dundee and Wishart's. Transfers of Solos between depots was common with Pensnett and Walsall becoming operators of them, albeit briefly in both cases. Withdrawals started in 2010; many found new homes with other operators but some went for scrap.

Travel West Midlands took delivery of 44 Optare Solos in 1999. They were 8.5m-long 27-seaters. Previous small buses had been Mercedes-Benz Varios. The four-track route number blind is an unusual feature. This is Halesowen in 2006.

OPTARE EXCEL

The Excel was bigger than the Solo, and the 35 delivered to Travel West Midlands in 1999 were L1070 models with 38 seats. The Excels were operated solely by Wolverhampton depot on local routes, and they rarely strayed beyond the town. Dudley was as far as they would venture.

Reliability of the Optare Excel was an issue from the start but Wolverhampton depot persevered with them and towards the end they had become a lot more reliable, but their fragile nature meant that

other buses, including step-entrance Volvo B10Bs and MCW Metrobuses, often replaced them on routes which should have been low-floor.

In 2002 the Excel fleet was boosted by the arrival of 14 L960s from Travel London. These were converted to single door layout and entered service briefly at Birmingham Central, but within two months had joined their larger cousins at Wolverhampton.

Seven others were moved to Dundee, but by late 2008 they had been transferred back south to TWM and not surprisingly Wolverhampton was

The first big orders for low-floor double-deckers saw 102 Volvo B7TLs entering service in 1999-2000. They had 74-seat Plaxton President bodies. This 2006 view in Birmingham shows the original livery carried by the Presidents.

the recipient of these too. All the ex-Dundee Excels carried the new National Express West Midlands livery, which sat rather well on these short buses. Of the larger Excels, only six gained the new NXWM livery.

Withdrawals began in 2011 with the short Excels being the first to go and by the end of that year all were gone. The first of the larger versions were withdrawn in 2012 and most had gone by the end of that year leaving just the seven in the new livery. Their time came in early 2013 when they were replaced by older B6LEs.

VOLVO B7TL/PLAXTON PRESIDENT

What was arguably the first standard low-floor double-deck type to enter service with Travel West Midlands were the 102 Plaxton President-bodied Volvo B7TLs which followed on from the Spectras in 1999-2000, taking fleet numbers from 4023 upwards.

The fleet was split between a number of garages when new, including Birmingham Central, which put the first 18 on Hagley Road services, Walsall, Acocks Green, Yardley Wood, Hockley and Perry Barr which had a large number Presidents for Sutton Lines services. One of the lesser-known services that the Presidents were used on when new was the Airlink

which saw five, 4120-24, fitted with dual-purpose seating, which involved adding a small headrest to the standard seat. Airlink was classed as an express service linking Birmingham city centre with the airport. The service was short-lived and the five Presidents ended up back with others in the fleet at Birmingham Central.

As with all the new low-floor buses, most of the routes the Presidents worked came with route branding in the form of different coloured roundels.

Like the Mercedes and Volvo B10Ls, the Presidents were swapped between depots on a regular basis. With more and more newer buses entering service at garages occupied by Presidents, many were quickly relegated to other services or transferred away.

Of interest amongst the depot allocations is that from 2007 the majority of the Presidents were allocated to Birmingham Central, with just small pockets at West Bromwich and Acocks Green. One plan was to make Birmingham Central a 100 per cent B7TL depot, however this plan wasn't to last too long with proposals to introduce tighter emissions controls in Birmingham city centre. With the emissions restrictions applying to the city centre only, many of the Presidents found a new home circling the city on the Outer Circle which they still do today, allocated to Acocks Green garage. ■

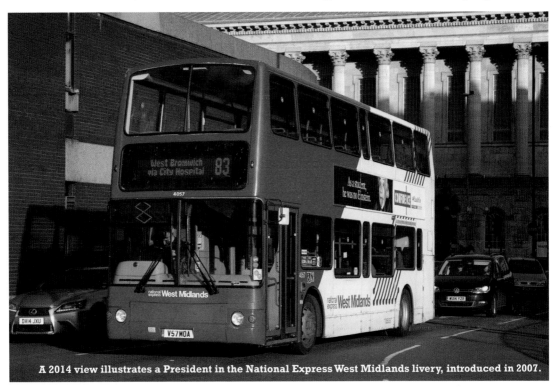

A 2014 view illustrates a President in the National Express West Midlands livery, introduced in 2007.

BRIGHTER OLYMPIANS

Bright new colours appeared on ECW-bodied Olympians which had once been standard NBC red or green, **Stewart J. Brown** illustrates a selection.

The standard National Bus Company double-decker of the 1980s was the Leyland Olympian with bodywork by ECW of Lowestoft. It could be seen the length and breadth of England and Wales, from United Auto in the north-east, to Western National in the south-west.

ECW supplied just over 1,000 bodies on Olympian chassis to NBC, and the vast majority were standard 77-seat buses delivered in unexciting poppy red or leaf green. There were a few coach-seated bodies, and a small number of proper coaches, including batches on long-wheelbase chassis for London commuter services. There was also one order from London Country, for 15 vehicles built to a similar specification to those supplied to London Country (and Bristol Omnibus) by Roe. The Roe body was slightly higher than that built by ECW and used different windscreens.

Most NBC Olympians had Gardner 6LXB engines.

While poppy red or leaf green were the colours applied for most NBC Olympians when they left the ECW paint shop, in later life a variety of much brighter colour schemes could be seen. ■

ABOVE: **The way things were. Most Leyland Olympians delivered to NBC were in poppy red or leaf green with a single band of white relief. Even by the standards of the 1980s this was not an exciting livery, as United Auto 226 (AEF 226Y) of 1983 shows. At least the red was bright; the same could not be said for NBC green. Between 1982 and 1985 United bought 68 Olympians.**

TOP RIGHT: **Three standard Olympians were delivered to East Yorkshire in 1984. Originally in poppy red, as seen on the United bus above, 532 (A532 OKH) is in Scarborough in 1991 after the company was privatised and had adopted a more sombre shade of red, relieved by grey. It has been fitted with high-backed seats.**

BOTTOM RIGHT: **In 1985 Crosville took five Olympians with 71 coach seats; B203 DTU passed to Midland Red North which in 1989 had taken over part of Crosville's operations. Both companies were at that tome part of the Drawlane group. For a time in the early 1990s Midland Red North adopted a retro look, harking back to the glory days of the original Midland Red business with all-over red and a traditional style of fleetname. Perhaps poppy red was better after all.**

LEFT: **Another Crosville Olympian which in later life swapped leaf green for brighter colours. A134 SMA of 1983 is seen in Leicester ten years later with Midland Fox, which acquired it in 1989 from Crosville Wales. It was later converted to open-top for Birmingham sightseeing tours.**

BELOW LEFT: **Towards the end of the NBC era the group relaxed its hitherto strict policy on liveries, and three coach-seated Olympians for Midland Red South were delivered in this eye-catching colour scheme. This is a 1990 view in Stratford when Midland Red South was part of Western Travel. When in NBC ownership the Olympians carried the double-N logo on the side panels below the first upper deck window.**

BELOW: **Lincolnshire Road Car specified coach seats on its only three new Olympians, delivered in 1985 in a non-standard coach livery. The company's bright post-privatisation livery is seen on 601 (B501 FFW) in Scunthorpe. It was still in service when Stagecoach bought Road Car in 2005.**

TOP RIGHT: There was a massive clear-out of double-deckers at Devon General, as the operation focussed on running high-frequency services with small buses. Southern National acquired this 1983 bus in 1990. It was photographed in Weymouth.

MIDDLE RIGHT: Half a dozen coach-seated Olympians were purchased by United Auto in 1985 including 267 (C267 XEF) seen in the colourful livery adopted by Tees & District, one of the privatised successors of United. Tees & District was set up in 1990 as part of Caldaire Holdings, which was briefly a major operator in the north-east of England and parts of Yorkshire.

BELOW LEFT: Ribble was a big user of ECW-bodied Olympians, building up a fleet of 80. 2173 (C173 ECK) was one of ten delivered in 1985 with coach seats for use on interurban services. It continued as an interurban vehicle after Ribble was bought by Stagecoach, here arriving in Manchester on the X43 from Colne. The X43 still exists today, but starts from Nelson and is run by Transdev using Volvo B9TLs with Wrightbus bodies.

BELOW RIGHT: County Motors of Lepton was a small business which for many years was owned jointly by Yorkshire Traction, Yorkshire Woollen and West Riding. It was taken over by Yorkshire Traction in 1968, but its livery was revived on a few vehicles some 20 years later, as shown by Yorkshire Traction Olympian 638 (A638 WDT) in Huddersfield in 1990.

Another former Ribble Olympian in Manchester, but in the ownership of Bee Line, part of the Drawlane organisation. The livery layout may be conventional, but the warm colours are attractive.

BELOW LEFT: **A number of former NBC Olympians were sold for further service by their privatised owners in the late 1980s and early 1990s. This Southend Transport Leyland Olympian, 256 (A110 FDL), had been new to Southern Vectis in 1984 as A701 DDL. It was fitted with coach seats in 1987 and bought by Southend in 1991 partly for use on the X1 London express service.**

TOP RIGHT: **Blackpool Transport purchased ten 1983-84 Olympians from Trent in 1996. They served their new owner well, running until 2012. 408 (A708 DAU) is in St. Annes soon after joining the Blackpool fleet, heading north for Blackpool and Fleetwood.**

MIDDLE RIGHT: **Spot the difference. Not all NBC Olympians were bodied by ECW. Both Bristol Omnibus and London Country selected Roe bodies which were slightly higher and featured the style of windscreen which had been used on Park Royal-bodied Atlanteans for NBC. The sharp-eyed will note that the lower deck windows are slightly deeper. On the standard ECW body the tops of the lower deck windows aligned with the top of the window on the emergency exit; they don't on the Roe body. This is a former Bristol bus is in service with Cheltenham & Gloucester's Stroud Valleys fleet. Bristol had 75 of these Roe-bodied Olympians.**

BELOW: **Very few British PSVs received Q-registrations, which are issued to vehicles of doubtful provenance or, as the DVLA more politely puts it 'vehicles whose age or identity is in doubt'. This Olympian was Leyland's prototype B45-01, complete with an NBC-style ECW body shell, but with a Bristol VR front panel. It is seen in Manchester, in the ownership of Stevensons.**

BESIDE THE SEASIDE

All photographs
by the author.

Bob Hind reflects on the joys
of coastal bus service.

L iving on an island there is one thing that is always guaranteed – spectacular coastal scenery and, whilst I may be a little biased, I believe there is only one way to enjoy the full splendour of our coastline and that is from the top of a double-decker bus (with or without its top in place).

Britain's bus companies provide plenty of opportunities for the many millions of visitors to our seaside resorts to take in the views from 15 feet in the air and some companies are a little more adventurous than others. Open-top vehicles are usually an excuse to roll out a 30-year-old Metrobus

for six weeks of the year and to keep it mothballed for the remainder in the hope that your local football team may, one day, win the cup.

But the regular tour buses seen in so many cities around the world nowadays have meant that passengers in the more provincial resorts expect a bit more sophistication. Travelling around this island's coastline I came across some wonderful and occasional weird examples of the industry doing its bit for the holiday trade.

Skegness would still be bracing but not quite the same if Stagecoach's Coastal Cruiser, adorned with cute sea lions, wasn't ploughing its way up and down the east coast between Ingoldmells, Fantasy Island, Butlins and the capital of this holiday paradise, Skeggy. Whilst not the most interesting piece of coastline, just taking in the Meccano-like architecture of the the fairgrounds and pleasure havens mixed with a wash of enthusiasm from your fellow passengers (have you ever seen unhappy holiday makers?) is worth the experience. Stagecoach produces a helpful Coastal Guide and the booklet lists 31 places of interest and 46 holiday camps. The east coast remains as popular as ever and, I suspect, most visitors don't want it to change.

In Skegness bus station, Stagecoach East's traditional open-top Dennis Trident prepares for its return trip along the Lincolnshire coast.

First Hampshire & Dorset's CoastlinX53 heading eastwards across a darkening Dorset countryside, operated by a Wrightbus Eclipse Gemini-bodied Volvo B9TL.

There were a couple of non-double-deck routes I just had to include in this jaunt around the seaside. Whilst normally operated by Optare Solos, a coastal route that really should be double-decked is Norfolk Green's Coasthopper, now owned by Stagecoach, which runs all the year round along East Anglia's north coast from Kings Lynn up to Hunstanton and across to Cromer. The hourly service is obviously a lifeline to those living in this part of Norfolk throughout the year, I shared my journey with a bunch of schoolkids, but for visitors to this strangely peaceful part of the English coastline, there is much to absorb. The sad and sometimes neglected Victorian seaside towns at Hunstanton and Cromer are the bookends to a piece of coast that is home to a string of charming villages and an endless list of attractive eating places. Wells-next-the-Sea is the prettiest of hamlets and for the more adventurous Sheringham has its railways, both real (Abellio Greater Anglia) and the voluntary North Norfolk railway quaintly nick-named the 'Poppy Line'.

The south coast has its riches of coastal bus services; in fact it seems unfair that 'the south' should have quite so many premier routes that tick every box when it comes to service, scenery and sea views. Just four routes can take you from Dover to Portsmouth, 140 miles of English seaside and countryside, with time to enjoy history, picture postcard views and chocolate box villages with occasional glimpses of the outline of the French coast.

Stagecoach provides these glorious opportunities firstly, with its Wave route 101 from Dover to Hastings. This hourly service clings to the English Channel for most of its three-hour route linking four of the famous Cinque Ports, Dover, Hythe, Romney

Brighton & Hove's Coaster route 12 heads from Brighton towards Eastbourne through beautiful Sussex countryside. The bus is an East Lancs-bodied Scania OmniDekka.

Go Ahead's Brighton & Hove subsidiary's Coaster is loading at the White Lion Hotel in Seaford on its way to Eastbourne.

and Hastings. The route also reminds passengers that this piece of coastline has often been our main defence, spending much of history repelling would-be invaders. Retired fortifications dot the beaches and the Defence Training Camp at Hythe, where sand dunes are edged by barbed wire, recall less happy times.

At Hastings, the 101 links with another Wave route, the 99, that continues the journey through to Eastbourne every 20 minutes. Continuing the invasion theme, visitors are reminded that they are now firmly in 1066 Country as the 99 passes through Battle and past Conquest Hospital. The landscape does become a little more sedate through the leafy suburbs of Bexhill-on-Sea before the route makes a stately entrance along the lengthy Eastbourne promenade.

A non-Stagecoach company bridges the 24-mile gap between Eastbourne and Brighton. Go Ahead's Brighton and Hove Coaster service 12, runs up to every 10 minutes up Beachy Head and on to Peacehaven and finally Brighton.

The real coastal prize waits in Churchill Square where the Stagecoach Coastline 700 can be found for its four-and-a-half hour journey to Portsmouth, amazingly every 20 minutes. The thoroughly modern (wi-fi and plush seats) service passes through a string of very English resorts including Worthing, Littlehampton, and Royal Bognor Regis. Its arrival at The Hard Interchange on the edge of Portsmouth harbour provides a fitting end to the nautical experiences along this part of south-east England. HMS Victory greets visitors from its mooring in the Historic Dockyard with a dignified sense that we are still ready to repel any unwanted invaders.

For those with even more stamina, but who are

ABOVE: **First's elderly 27-year-old Alexander RV-bodied Volvo Citybus open-topper completes the three-hour tour of Land's End from Penzance It is arriving at the Malakoff bus station in St. Ives.**

BELOW: **A Scania with ADL Enviro400 body on the impressive Stagecoach South Coastliner 700 waits in The Hard Interchange at Portsmouth, almost at the westerly end of its 260-minute journey.**

rewarded with the most breathtaking scenery through Dorset and Devon, First Wessex's Jurassic CoastlinX53 from Poole to Exeter takes some beating. Another four-and-a-half hour journey, but longer in the summer, it only manages two or three complete trips a day. However the route manages to combine the charm of Georgian architecture in Weymouth with the film location popularity of Lyme Regis where visitors still search for fossils amidst 200 million years of archeology.

Conventional, traditional and old, visiting Lands End by First's open-topper may be disappointing from a bus enthusiast's point of view but seems to be appropriate for, after all, this is only the end of the country and the three-hour trip, if you do the extremely slow full circle is quite boring after the first 20 minutes. It can also be quite chilling if you risk the Atlantic winds from the open top deck for any length of time. But if you are in this part of Cornwall in the summer season, it should be compulsory to experience an old-fashioned open-topper to the furthest point west of our island.

Getting to Lynmouth in North Devon, for the most unusual of coastal bus services, is a challenge in itself. The water fed funicular from Lynton down the almost vertical cliff to Lynmouth is unique to these islands and worth the journey to North Devon. But the opportunity to travel onwards to Minehead on a single-deck half-open-topper was certainly not to be missed. Quantock Motor Services Scenic Coastal bus service had 20 seats open to the elements and 25 inside with the heating. The summer route climbs steeply from Lynmouth on to Exmoor and deep into Lorna Doone country. The views south across the moor and north across the Bristol Channel are certainly captivating and this unconventional bus accommodates all tastes.

The Cymru Coastliner, which for so long ran between Caernarfon and Chester along the North Wales coast, has haunted its successors who try to emulate the nostalgia without offering the real thing. A three-and-a-half-hour journey along the North Wales coast, through the traditional Victorian resorts of Llandudno, Colwyn Bay and the caravan parks of

Definitely not a bus, but the quickest descent between Lynton and Lynmouth is by the 125-year-old water-powered Lynton and Lynmouth Cliff Railway.

ABOVE: **The author's favourite, Quantock Motor Services' coastal half-and-half bus waiting at Lynmouth for its morning trip along the North Devon coast to Minehead. It is a 1997 Alexander-bodied Volvo B10M which had been new to Stagecoach Manchester.**

RIGHT: **Arriva Cymru's 21st-century version of the famous Cymru Coastliner on the Chester to Rhyl leg of the service, operated by a Wrightbus Eclipse Gemini 2DL.**

Rhyl and Prestatyn, now takes over six hours by three different routes and whilst a modern, smart fleet still provides the views, for the older passengers, like me, it's not quite the same.

Arriva's X5 squeezes between Snowdonia and the Menai Straits for much of its journey between Caernarfon and Llandudno. Views of Anglesey and the Great Orme in the distance provide a spectacular backcloth as the bus clings to the coast. The ancient castle at Conwy looks out across the estuary and, sadly, I suspect at the redundant Crosville garage at Llandudno Junction.

Llandudno still bustles with week-enders and day trippers but if you want to continue the Coastliner experience you have to change here on to service 12 for the busy section through Colwyn Bay, up Penmaen Head then descending into Abergele for the endless final straight run through chalets, caravans, amusements and bars into a perpetually forlorn Rhyl.

ABOVE: **Another elderly open-topper, near Prestatyn, in the shape of a one-time London Buses Leyland Olympian operated by Arriva Cymru between Talacre and Pensarn.**

RIGHT: **Not quite on the seaside, but Stagecoach Ribble's Morecambe and Wise bus, seen here in Lancaster's bus station, sends the right message to holidaymakers.**

The third leg from Rhyl to Chester leaves behind the holiday homes of Prestatyn, Talacre and Gronant, where you may just see a conventional open topper providing a seasonal link. It passes through a string of small towns that all once had a purpose (mining) but now just provide some relief as we approach the end of the line at Chester. For long considered the North Wales 'capital' despite lying four miles inside England, Chester has retained its charm although never being able to cope with an excess of visitors.

There really should be a properly-marketed coastal bus services campaign as so much can be offered to visitors to our shore for such little cost. The view

from the top of a double-deck is by far the best way to experience our spectacular coastline any time of the year and it remains a part of the bus industry that is constantly undersold.

The irony is, that whilst many European cities rely on expensive tour buses to promote their offerings, these isles have regular local bus services that do the same thing better and more frequently at a fraction of the cost. ■

The Manchester Front

From 1957 until the end of production in 1971 front-engined Daimlers used a glass fibre grille named after the first operator to receive it, Manchester City Transport. **Geoff Mills** illustrates a selection.

ABOVE: **Daimler's new-look front was first seen on a batch of 30 Daimler CVG6s delivered to Manchester City Transport in 1957. This design was unique to Daimler; previously the company had used the Birmingham-style grille which was also fitted to Crossley and Guy chassis. This Burlingham-bodied bus is seen in the ownership of the Selnec PTE in 1972. The bus alongside has a non-standard grille.**

LEFT: **Derby Corporation was a long-standing Daimler customer and between 1961 and 1966 took 47 CVG6s with 65-seat Roe bodies, and then switched to Roe-bodied Fleetlines. This is a 1961 bus. The fluted badge at the top of the grille echoed the design of the traditional Daimler radiator used on both buses and cars.**

1

Northampton Corporation, like Derby, favoured Roe-bodied CVG6s, albeit with a different style of body featuring deeper windows on the lower deck. In 1966 it took five. 256 (ENH 256D) is one of a long line of Roe-bodied Daimlers with an unbroken run of fleet numbers from 170 in 1949 to 267 in 1968.

2

Ten CVG6s were delivered to Swindon Corporation in 1961 and had bodies built by Roe, but to the designs of Roe's sister company, Park Royal. This one is seen when new, complete with informative but difficult-to-read destination display.

3

A wider grille, with 12 vertical slats instead of ten, was used on 30ft-long chassis, which had a different frame. This CVG6LX/30 with 70-seat Roe body was one of four for Huddersfield in 1964. This is a 1969 view.

4

Relatively few independent operators were buying front-engined Daimlers in the 1960s. This CVG6LX/30 with 74-seat Northern Counties body was new to A1 of Ardrossan in 1962.

5

The wider grille was later used on all CVG6s, regardless of length, as shown by this Alexander-bodied bus which was one of eight for Aberdeen Corporation in 1965. Aberdeen was the most northerly buyer of CVG6s with Manchester fronts, and its 1965 buses were the last for a Scottish operator. In 1966 Aberdeen switched to Fleetlines.

6

In 1966 Doncaster Corporation took its last CVG6s, and like many other municipal buyers then changed to the Fleetline. There were six in 1966, with 62-seat Roe bodies.

TOP RIGHT: **Bradford Corporation took one batch of Daimlers with new-look fronts, 15 CVG6LX/30s bodied by Neepsend which entered service in 1966. Bradford also bought AEC Regents and Leyland Titans in the 1960s, and later in the decade divided its orders between Leyland Atlanteans and Daimler Fleetlines.**

Most, but not all, Daimlers with Manchester fronts were CVG6s or CVG6LX/30s with six-cylinder Gardner engines and semi-automatic transmissions. Burton-on-Trent Corporation specified Gardner 5LW engines and manual gearboxes in its Daimlers in the 1960s. There were 21 CCG5s with 61-seat Massey bodies, delivered between 1963 and 1968. This is a 1966 bus, photographed soon after delivery.

ARRIVA North East
A RISING STAR

Arriva offers two premium brands, Sapphire and MAX. The latter was launched in September 2014 as a less extravagant version of Sapphire. Refurbished for the role, is a 2009 Wrightbus Gemini 2.

Arriva North East has changed dramatically in recent years. **Graeme Palmer** tells the story.

All photographs by the author

Arriva North East has seen quite a transformation over the past decade. If we go back to 2005, the business was the second beneficiary of Operation Overdrive, a programme designed by Arriva to raise service standards. Gillingham in Kent was the first depot to be given the treatment, and received a substantial 61 new vehicles. Arriva North East then seized on the Arriva Southern Counties disposal list, taking around 15 MetroRiders. After being scattered across the company on arrival, a number of these were later used to 'upgrade' a Middlesbrough to Redcar service from a 15-minute to a 10-minute headway, but with low-floor DAF SB120s being replaced by step-entry buses. This was perhaps typical of Arriva North East at the time.

Following the success of Operation Overdrive in the Medway Towns it was announced in 2005 that Arriva North East was to experience Operation Overdrive round two. The company had received just 15 new vehicles since 2000 - nine DAF DB250s in 2001, three Wright Commander-bodied SB200s in 2003, and two Mini

Operation Overdrive saw 1998 Plaxton Prestige-bodied DAF SB220s being refurbished. 4073 (S715 KRG) is seen in Durham in September 2005 soon after being treated.

Pointer Darts in 2003-04. It was therefore welcome news that 27 new vehicles were to join the fleet – 25 for Durham and two for Darlington. Durham had an allocation of around 62, so the investment represented a replacement of around 40 per cent of the fleet. As part of the programme, seven Mini Pointer Darts and 17 DAF SB220s were also refurbished.

The Overdrive project at Durham always struck me as being somewhat half-hearted. While in the Medway Towns, Gillingham depot operated almost all of the mileage in the area, the same was not the case in Durham City where Peterlee and Bishop Auckland depots both made a significant contribution to the city network.

The two buses for Darlington were Volvo B7TLs bought for its share of the 723 trunk service linking Darlington, Durham and Newcastle. But while Darlington introduced new buses for its share of the route, Durham replaced 2001-build DAF DB250 double-deckers with refurbished seven-year old SB220 single-deckers.

In Medway, Operation Overdrive very much gave the impression Arriva had thrown all of its money into one pot; in Durham the feeling was much more that a few new buses had been thrown in to an otherwise unloved

fleet. Indeed, glossy publicity was absent so I doubt the target audience knew Operation Overdrive ever happened, nor what it involved.

The lack of impact of Operation Overdrive in Durham was compounded by the many months it took to brand the new vehicles. The new and refurbished vehicles were launched with little fanfare and, belatedly, half-hearted branding was applied to many of the new Scania OmniCitys to promote their use on two local services and on the X1 to Newcastle and Middlesbrough.

The investment in the fleet was somewhat cancelled out by the decision in 2004/05 to send 16 Dart SLFs and two step-entry examples to Arriva Cymru in exchange for 18 step-entry Varios. These followed eight Dart SLFs that left for Cymru in 2003, these having been replaced by several resuscitated step-entrance MAN 11.190s with Optare Vecta bodies. A couple of town routes in Darlington lost low-floor vehicles while Bishop Auckland

The Optare Prisma, built on a Mercedes-Benz O405 chassis, was a fairly rare type. One of the biggest users was Tees & District, which took 25 in 1995. This one is seen in Arriva ownership in Stokesley High Street in 2006.

In retaliation against Go-Ahead's Bargain Bus, Arriva registered competing service X21 between Newcastle and Durham. A Mini Pointer Dart exits Durham bus station in December 2006 with X21 branding.

Among the new buses delivered in 2009 were Wrightbus Pulsar-bodied VDL SB200s. 1418 (NK09 EJG) pauses at Ramshaw terminus in February 2010 before returning to Bishop Auckland.

The recast Darlington network in 2009 saw five routes gaining brand names, illustrated by Alexander-bodied Dennis Dart 1677 (P634 PGP) on Branksome Boomerang service 2. The Dart had been new to Selkent in 1996.

The Optare Vecta-bodied MAN 11.190 was another fairly rare model. 1553 (M502 AJC) was new to Crosville Wales in 1995 and is seen in Saltburn in 2009, nearing the end of its life.

Arriva North East was the only significant customer for the Turkish-built Temsa Avenue, taking 20 in 2010. One loads in Guisborough.

progressively lost all 20 of its Dart SLFs so, once again, passengers on some routes saw low-floor buses being replaced by vehicles with entrance steps.

Things were to get much worse over the two years that followed. In 2006, Arriva bought Go North East's Bishop Auckland operations with no exchange of vehicles. An opportunity existed to recast the network and invest in the fleet. Limited recasting came, but Arriva North East felt it would be a much better idea to buy whatever was cheap on the Arriva UK Bus disposals list. In came four step-entry Darts from Yorkshire, ten Volvo B6s from North West (a type the company had never operated,

and that had become renowned for poor reliability), plus six elderly Leyland Olympians, two newer examples and six DAF DB250s from London and Southern Counties. The B6s almost inevitably proved to be chronically unreliable, with lost mileage at Bishop Auckland being a clear concern. A number of these incoming vehicles did not initially gain destination blinds; consequently they displayed route numbers only. Some vehicles didn't even display route numbers, and instead had boards stuck to the inside of the windscreen.

The B6 problem was resolved in 2007 when 11 R-registered Dart SLFs came in from London, although Bishop Auckland initially only got four of them, with the other B6s replaced by internal cascades.

In North Yorkshire, the core half-hourly Richmond to Darlington service was soon doubled in 2005 to every 15 minutes but downgraded to MetroRider operation. This was followed in 2006 by the closure of Richmond depot. Most services were transferred to Darlington depot.

In 2007, service 723 (now running between Durham and Darlington only and no longer a joint operation with Go-Ahead) gained similar enhancements, going from every 30 minutes to every 15 minutes but with the Overdrive-specification Volvo B7TLs removed. It became normal for life-expired step-entry Darts and MetroRiders to run alongside the refurbished low-floor SB220s.

In 2013, Arriva paid tribute to 100 years of United Automobile Services. This Alexander-bodied Volvo B7TL is wearing an imaginative commemorative 'zip' livery in which the rear part of the bus is in United red.

Operating standards ailed on Teesside too. In 2006, Arriva recast the network on Teesside in response to continued decline in ridership, under the banner Viva Tees Valley. No new vehicles were brought in. This aimed to bring higher frequencies to many corridors. While the 15-minute headway X3/X4 (Middlesbrough to Easington) that came in with this network relaunch has been a continued success, overall the new network was poorly received and most importantly failed to halt the decline in ridership. It did not deliver the stable, sustainable bus network promised. Further service cuts came only a year later and more changes and cuts have followed.

In summer 2007, serious maintenance and reliability concerns arose at Redcar, leading to the hiring in of three Blackpool Transport MetroRiders and two dealer-stock Ikarus-bodied DAFs. This, along with the desire to convert service 63 (Middlesbrough to Redcar) to low-floor, led to a fleet upgrade at Redcar. However, rather than buy new buses, Arriva North East shuffled its fleet. SB220s at Loftus were exchanged for Mercedes-Benz saloons, while a further signal that Operation Overdrive at Durham might have failed came as the X1 was stripped of some of its Scania OmniCitys, these

In 2014 a park-and-ride service was introduced in Whitby using two all-over white Optare Solos. High ridership has seen one of the Solos replaced by a refurbished ex-London Wrightbus-bodied B7TL in a smart purple and silver livery.

Arriva was quick to respond when Go North East started encroaching on its Newcastle to Ashington expresses in 2009. Scania saloons were painted red and branded 'Northumbria Express'. Arriva's route largely lives on, now numbered X20. The Scania is a 1995 L113CRL with East Lancs body, new to Northumbria Motor Services.

Arriva North East was one of the pioneer users of the group's Sapphire brand. In 2014 the company bought seven ADL Enviro400s for the X21/X22 between Ashington and Newcastle. This is Ashington bus station.

going to Redcar in exchange for Mercedes-Benz. Perhaps unsurprisingly, service reliability and lost mileage rose at Loftus depot, with the Ikarus-bodied DAFs remaining to help out there.

At Darlington, meanwhile, vehicle presentation declined when the Feethams depot bus wash broke down. Buses were routinely seen around the town for months with what became trademark dirty bumpers. Despite 'dirty bumper syndrome' gripping the town, Arriva took over Stagecoach's under-performing Darlington operations in the summer of 2007, with this takeover bringing in the 28 step-entry Darts that had been running the routes.

In Northumberland, the demands of Cobalt Business Park on North Tyneside saw route branding on ex-Cymru Varios for two routes serving Cobalt. This was simply tacked on to the paintwork they'd come with from Cymru – further evidence that vehicle presentation was ailing. In 2007 another Viva network relaunch was carried out. Many routes were renumbered to make things 'easier to understand'. The signature of this relaunch, meanwhile, was a complicated 13-hour interworking cycle of various minibus routes around Cramlington and North Tyneside. Again, this relaunch was unsuccessful and has been followed by further

major network changes in subsequent years, with some of the changes involved being similarly ill-advised.

Overall, Arriva North East was in quite a state. Public and political faith in the company was deteriorating. Go North East (rejuvenated under the management of the late Peter Huntley) was starting to sense blood. During 2006-07, Go North East developed a new competitive Cobalt Clipper service. New Bargain Bus services X42/X43 were launched in direct competition with Arriva's flagship Newcastle to Blyth expresses. The Bishop Auckland to Newcastle service was doubled to half-hourly and absorbed into the Angel brand. A Pink Panthers city service was launched in Durham, though this proved unsuccessful and so was short-lived. Arriva retaliated with a route-branded Newcastle to Durham express, numbered X21, plus two defensive routes in North Tyneside and south-east Northumberland.

With poor operating standards now joined by the backdrop of competition concerns, Arriva finally decided a fresh approach was needed, and towards the end of 2007 in came a new managing director, Jonathan May, to raise the company's game. The previous management had ordered 13 ADL Enviro400s for the X31/X32/X33 Ashington express network. However, faced with the need to respond to Go North East's encroachments, six of these Enviro400s were diverted to the 308, linking Blyth, Whitley Bay and Newcastle, which was relaunched as Coastliner.

One of May's first actions was to oversee a recasting of Darlington's town network in the summer of 2008. The network had teething problems, particularly with the North Road corridor being left with fewer buses, and with unreliability on the country routes involved. However, largely the same network remains in place today, so clearly this network relaunch was more successful than those witnessed in Bishop Auckland, Teesside and Northumberland/North Tyneside. The

new Darlington network was supported with 28 new Optare Solos.

With a further 23 Solos going to Peterlee and Durham depots, appropriate scales of vehicle investment were finally back on the menu. After Darlington, May's next project was to simplify North Northumberland services into three routes with enhanced service levels and a new Coasts & Castles brand.

In Northumberland, Go North East had continued to increase its competitive Cobalt Clipper and Bargain Bus services throughout 2008, along with its presence on the Coast Road corridor. In early 2009, Arriva and Go North East parted ways on the 308, this having been a joint service since before deregulation. Arriva registered to run the full 15-minute headway, while Go North East's 308 became a half-hourly Bargain Bus service. VDL SB200s were hired in to cover the balance of the 308's peak vehicle requirement at the start of 2009, these going on to fulfil various roles with the company before departing in mid-2010.

Sapphire was launched on Teesside with a fleet of Wrightbus StreetLites in September 2014. Brand new 1556 (NK14 GGO) awaits departure from Middlesbrough.

The Coasts & Castles branding is now restricted to the X18. The route was relaunched in November 2014 under the MAX brand with new Enviro400s. 7532 is shown here at Regent's Centre.

The X93 is now a MAX route with double-deck Volvos but as a prelude to this, the 2013 summer season saw Scania OmniCitys gain Seasider branding for the route which links Middlesbrough, Whitby and Scarborough. 4655 (NK05 GXJ) is seen here in Guisborough, notably on the wrong route.

In late 2008, it was decided the Mercedes-Benz saloons were too unreliable for Durham's lengthy X1 service. SB220s and step-entry Scania saloons took charge of the route, with the Mercedes-Benz saloons consequently making their way back to Redcar and Loftus. Around the same time, the decision was taken to close Loftus depot and in January 2009 its service output was shared between Redcar, Whitby outstation and Stockton. Many of the more unreliable vehicles at Loftus ended up back at Redcar, and service reliability at Redcar and at Whitby continued to decline.

There was further investment in 2009 with the arrival of 57 Wrightbus Pulsars, eight ADL Enviro400s and 15 VDL DB300s. Towards the end of 2009, 12 of the Pulsars were delivered to Redcar, with 20 Temsa Avenues following in early 2010. With this investment, Redcar was finally able to rid itself of the unreliable MAN 11.190s and Mercedes-Benz saloons that had plagued service quality for several years.

There were three depot closures at Arriva North East in 2010, at Peterlee, Alnwick and Bishop Auckland. A new depot opened in Durham to replace Peterlee and Bishop Auckland, though it was December 2012 before it had been expanded sufficiently to also absorb the allocation of Durham's Waddington Street depot. The closure of Bishop Auckland depot initially proved very problematic, with some service reliability concerns. Subsequent service changes, including a number of further cuts, have resolved this though, and Bishop Auckland now enjoys a reduced but reliable bus network from Arriva.

The Go North East competition problem was resolved in 2010. In 2009, Go North East had further encroached on Arriva turf with an X41 Ashington to Newcastle Bargain Express. Arriva was a lot more on the ball this time, and quickly responded with a duplicate X30 Northumbria Express, running five minutes ahead of the X41. The X41 performed poorly and in 2010 a compromise was reached, with Arriva sacrificing Hexham depot in exchange for Go North East's

Ashington base, enabling Arriva to regain full control of its lucrative Blyth and Ashington express corridors. Go North East has made further competitive encroachments since, but some of these have seen limited success. Indeed, Go North East's express between Bishop Auckland, Darlington and Middlesbrough did not last, despite use of the historically popular OK name. Arriva's quick launch of a competitive X1 service clearly helped to ensure Go North East's effort would be short-lived. Having launched the Tynedale Express in September 2013 in competition with the Newcastle to Hexham section of Arriva's service 685, Go North East now seems to have cooled on the competitive strategy in favour of retaining focus on its traditional work.

Investment has steadily continued at Arriva North East since the group was taken over in 2010 by Deutsche Bahn. Arriva North East now shares a management team with Arriva Yorkshire, headed by Nigel Featham, and the company has improved remarkably in the years since. The days of sweeping service cuts, failed Viva network relaunches and regular knee-jerk fleet movements seem to be over, with the agenda now firmly set on marketing routes effectively and increasing ridership.

Arriva North East was one of the test-beds for Arriva's Sapphire brand. At the time, County Durham had experienced one of the sharpest year-on-year declines in bus ridership in England. Service 7 (the current incarnation of the aforementioned 723) between Darlington and Durham was chosen for the concept. The buses were Wrightbus-bodied VDL SB200s which offer free wi-fi, at-seat power sockets and next-stop audio announcements with supporting digital screens. Drivers were specially selected for Sapphire service 7 and given a smart purpose-designed uniform. A money-back guarantee was also introduced should a customer be left dissatisfied. Performance figures exceeded DB's expectations, with service 7 achieving over 10 per cent growth in the first nine months of Sapphire operation.

The success of service 7 convinced Arriva North East that this was the way forward and in 2014, Teesside services X3 and X4 (Middlesbrough to Easington) and 5 (Middlesbrough to Loftus) were revised with an increased peak vehicle requirement and relaunched under the Sapphire brand with a fleet of 24 Wrightbus StreetLites supplemented by two refurbished VDL SB200s. Ashington to Newcastle express services X21/X22 also joined the Sapphire brand. Healthy growth has been achieved on the Teesside routes, although figures are a little more conservative for the X21/X22.

Encouraged by the success of its new approach, Arriva North East and Arriva Yorkshire developed a less luxurious version of Sapphire, branded as MAX. The MAX vehicles have e-leather seats, free wi-fi and a MAX uniform for the drivers, but at-seat power sockets and next stop announcements are not usually included. Blyth services X10/X11 were the first MAX routes launched at the end of summer 2014. The plan was always to roll this out on most interurban expresses across Arriva North East and so far this has seen the brand expanded onto Northumberland routes 14/X14, X15 and X18 which run from Newcastle to Morpeth and Berwick-on-Tweed; Darlington inter-urban routes X1, X26/X27 and X66, coastal service X93, and the Middlesbrough – Durham – Newcastle service, now numbered X12.

The X93 is itself an example of the company's transformation. After years of neglect and poor service reliability with a fleet of ageing single-deck vehicles, the X93 had in 2011 been the focus of a Seasider branding effort using OmniCitys. These compounded capacity problems and were replaced by larger Enviro400s, which were branded as SightSeeker for the 2013 summer season with a supporting TV and radio advertisement campaign. However, poor reliability led to the Enviro400s being replaced temporarily by ex-London B7TLs. The launch of brand new MAX-specification vehicles marks the conclusion of this route's transformation from unreliability and neglect to becoming a flagship service the company can be proud to associate its name with.

The MAX revolution is set to continue with refurbishment of further vehicles to add Blyth - Newcastle services X4/X5, and Amble – Ashington – Newcastle services 20/X20 to the MAX brand. Sapphire will expand too, and it would seem Sapphire has succeeded where Operation Overdrive failed, as 2015 saw the Sapphire brand being rolled out on Durham services 6 (to Bishop Auckland) and 22/24 (to Peterlee and Sunderland/Hartlepool). The continued success of Sapphire on service 7 will also see five new ADL Enviro400s displacing the SB200s on the busiest journeys.

Green Bus funding saw Volvo B5LH hybrids and gas-powered MAN EcoCitys join the fleet in 2013. Gas buses remain rare in the UK. Arriva's smart Eco livery is used on these vehicles, as shown by an MAN in Darlington Town Centre, photographed when new.

Arriva North East has embraced alternative technologies too. In 2013, ten Volvo B5LH hybrids arrived for Coastliner service 308, launched in Arriva's attractive Eco livery with an 'It's alive, it's electric' TV, radio and on-vehicle advertising campaign.

In Darlington, 11 gas-powered MAN EcoCity vehicles arrived, deployed on three town services. The success of these led to a further three dealer stock examples arriving in 2014. Arriva North East has also been a big buyer of StreetLite Micro Hybrids, with those not deployed on MAX and Sapphire routes going into the Eco livery. The Eco-liveried examples can be found on Ashington's service 35, Coastliner service 306 and Sunderland to Hartlepool service 23.

In their Sapphire, MAX and Eco livery, Arriva North East has established three effective brands that collectively market the stable backbone of the company's network. It paints the picture that these routes are here to stay and that this is a company now pushing for growth, not managing decline.

Beyond the three core brands, Arriva has also worked with the NHS to improve hospital links on Tyneside, with route branding promoting the improved services that have resulted from this partnership.

Timetable publicity has also been improved. Stylish Best Impressions-designed leaflets are produced in a uniform style for the MAX and Sapphire services. As well as promoting the special features of the vehicles, a range of well-designed maps are included to show the overall route and also routes and stop locations in major towns. These are complemented by text promoting the selling points of that location, be it shopping, beaches or cultural attractions. Sample fares are promoted in many MAX and Sapphire leaflets too.

The standard timetable design has been revamped, with shading making timetables easier to read than the previous all-white design. Across all timetables, Arriva North East uses colour-coding to highlight what days they cover – turquoise for Monday to Friday, blue for Saturday and green for Sunday.

Arriva North East has also fully embraced the technological age, through the Arriva Bus App. This incorporates a trip planner, timetables and a live 'real time' bus map, enabling people to see where their bus is. M-tickets are sold through the app – a concept Arriva was an early convert to. On social media, Arriva North East has for some time been active on Facebook and Twitter.

Arriva North East's efforts have not gone unnoticed, with its Blyth depot being runners-up for national depot of the year at the 2013 UK Bus Awards, and winning the bronze award in this category in 2014. Among the praises were a low lost mileage of 0.26 per cent, strong punctuality standards of 87 per cent, the 'It's alive, it's electric' campaign, high customer and employee satisfaction, good motivation among staff, 100 per cent pass rate for VOSA annual tests and active engagement in local community and charity initiatives.

From being one of the industry's poorest adverts for deregulated bus operation, Arriva North East really has emerged in the last few years to become one of the industry's unsung market leaders. ∎

A brief Breton break

PLUS A NANCY NOTION AND A CAEN CAPER

Robert E. Jowitt takes cross-Channel ferries for short dashes to France.

All photographs by the author.

All my life I have known this large picture, through some six moves over as many decades, until a year or so ago, my son Robin, for 20 years as familiar with it as I, looked at it perhaps more closely than hitherto, and asked, 'Is that just a fairytale, or is it a real place?'

'That is an etching by Axel Haig of the Mont St. Michel,' I replied, 'in Normandy... nearly Brittany...'

'Then let's go there!'

A plan enhanced for me by the fact that residing since 2013 on the Channel shore I can witness the passage of Brittany Ferries, usually the handsome Bretagne, en route to and from St Malo. Straight away Robin started booking tickets while I studied

guide books for hotels... and the history of St Malo tramways, finished more than half a century ago...

This was not the first time Robin and I had plotted a French dash. In March 2009 we had sailed out overnight on Brittany's Mont St, Michel from Portsmouth to Ouistreham, to return the next night, with a day in Caen. I had been in Caen 20 years before when ageing Saviem standard SC10s were still active, and subsequently my daughter had worked there, on some sort of scholastic exchange notion, in a solicitor's office, where much of the business was litigation about people who had injured themselves falling foul of the construction of the new 'tramway'. In 2007 I had studied the new 'tramway' in Nancy, and now Robin and I could inspect the Caen version.

It is worth noting that several French books hymning the re-introduction of trams into French cities eschew entirely any mention of Nancy or Caen, and in truth these are not trams as on other modern systems, though widely hailed as such on postcards and traffic signs. The vehicles in both places are very similar, and both run on rubber-tyred bus wheels and use a central 'third rail'. The major visible difference is that while Nancy has trolleybus type poles, Caen uses half-pantographs. I will not here examine this further, but rumour suggests both systems are to be replaced in the next few years

by true trams; sensible, if a loss to admirers of the bizarre.

Robin and I reached three out of the four Caen termini. Certain sections were not without merit, with some steep gradients through typical architecture, and a fine semi-circular over-all roof at one terminus. Other lengths were lugubrious French suburbia. In the centre we spent much time in cafés, imbibing not only mild alcohol but the spirit of French life, the whims and habits of customers and passers-by. We also visited the bus enquiry office, where we wanted timetables for future visits to Normandy Beaches.

Homeward bound in the bar of the Mont St. Michel I studied the timetables, for next time…

Next time was actually five years later, and not beaches but St. Malo, St. Michel our goal. Thus we boarded Bretagne in a grey Portsmouth evening.

BELOW: **Rear off-side, in Nancy (left) with interesting trolleybus-overhead standards, and in Caen (right) with the 'points' which lead the vehicles on and off the electrified section for auxiliary-powered depot journeys.**

Front off-side in Caen (above) descending one of several steep gradients past a fine café, and in Nancy (right) with a good example of Alsace art-nouveau architecture.

Woken early we hastened on deck to view a sensational prospect of rocky islets, lighthouses here and there, and, under sinister stormy clouds, the cliffs of Dinard with a few gleams of bright sun and verily the ramparts and towers and chimneys of St. Malo. So long had I been looking at guide books and maps, and here was the reality, just as promised!

Down the gangway to passport control, and walked along the quay to Porte St. Vincent and our nearby hotel. We took coffee on the terrace, then sallied up onto the walls, which is of course a St. Malo must with magnificent maritime views, and back to the bus terminus by Porte St. Vincent.

With leaflets on some local buses and trains we discovered the stop for the number 8 bus, which we wanted and which for no very good reason that I could see halted in a confusingly different spot than the more regular 1, 2 and 3. We duly boarded the 8, bought day tickets, and traversed streets of magnificent turn-of-the-century villas, even a century later many in fine order, the whole way most entertaining. At Rotheneuf to the celebrated Rochers Sculptés, of which I had known some long time, and wished to inspect.

While waiting for the bus onwards I was engaged in conversation by a good lady in the adjacent house, busy over her geraniums, who told me a couple waiting for a bus to St. Malo were waiting on this side of the road while the stop for St. Malo was opposite. I assured her we were bound for Cancale, and when she doubted

this possibility I further assured her that the summer timetable had just started and that a bus for Cancale would soon appear. I then congratulated her on her geraniums and we agreed that such toil is endless. And the 8 appeared.

Onwards, past many trim pseudo-rustic villas and many glimpses of bays and shores and headlands to Pointe de Grouin, whence we turned south, and Robin immediately sighted Mont St. Michel, far across the bay. Descended through thriving but not interesting Cancale to La Houle, (site of tram terminus), to eat good crepes in esplanade café.

I wanted to catch a 7, up to the terminus of Ville ès Gris (shown on the map in the timetable but – for heaven's sake why? – not given timings in the pages) because I hoped the bus would engage the erstwhile tramway gradient up above les Roches Noires. The bus stop time-table remedied the defects of its paper companion. When the 7 appeared, however, the driver had doubts about conveying us, and two ladies in apparent distress, up to Ville ès Gris. If we wanted St. Malo we should wait down here until he had gone up and turned at Ville ès Gris and come back. I insisted we wanted to go to Ville ès Gris first, and come back with

him after. He finally agreed to this but that he would put us off the bus at Ville ès Gris until he started back.

The ladies in distress were left by the stop to wait his return, we headed south, but, after an enticing vision of the former tramway gradient, took a short cut up to Ville ès Gris, and were duly dumped in a quite picturesque wooden bus shelter, of which there are several in this region. The driver had threatened that Ville ès Gris would be more boring than La Houle, and in this he was correct, but after doing his waybill for a few minutes he let us back on the bus for another ten, until we harked back down to La Houle, to pick up one of the ladies in distress. After passionate embraces the other remained in La Houle.

On the return journey Robin very soon fell asleep, and I must admit he didn't miss much, several miles of uninspiring hinterland, and, after a pair of fine water towers, Paramé suburbia and industry. On arrival at la gare de St. Malo, where the 7 finished I stupidly did not twig that the 1, 2 or 3 would serve onwards. Sensible damsel in bus enquiry office provided this answer and also I garnered some subsequently useful timetables. Thus back to Porte St. Vincent, or, as it is known on bus maps, Intra-Muros.

A Heuliez GX327 of Keolis at the Intra-Muros terminus at St. Malo, with spats partly covering the front wheels.

My readers may complain that of the day round St. Malo I have described only the routes and our journeyings, and nothing of the buses themselves, all Keolis-operated. Verily I can find little to say, and though we spent a while watching them at Intra-Muros I was not enthralled. I think the ones we experienced on the 8 and 7 were completely un-noteworthy models some few years of age.

On arrival I had very soon found a leaflet on Rance cruises and from same had ascertained that this Wednesday was the only day a cruise to Dinan operated. I had promised us this so bought tickets from the booking office on the Cale de Dinan where the maiden advised us that the boat had no refreshments, so we stocked up with wine and beer and sustenance from an amiable supermarket in Rue de Dinan.

The boat journey up La Rance is decried by certain guide-books as being over-exalted by other guide books. Arriving in Dinan we decided against immediate return on the boat – though the guide-book assured us that the river looks quite different the other way - for we wanted a little time to explore, and the return coach trip, as alternative included in the ticket, is, one has to admit, much quicker, if very much less enchanting.

The coach was mundanely modern. The driver, on the other hand, was notable for a completely shaven head and moustachios projecting an inch or two over his upper lip and hanging down either side of his mouth at least half-a-foot.

Next day started with a train to Pontorson. In the station yard was a bus of the sort – Citaro K - which should suit, but it had that familiar look of a bus which isn't going anywhere. Sundry parties assembled including a young girl with a cage containing a guinea pig which she now and then took from its container and cuddled in thoroughly French young girl style – a rash performance, I would have thought, in the station yard. Then a twin sister to the parked bus hove in and, our tickets accepted, headed north for le Mont.

Pilgrims originally crossed the sands at low tide to reach the holy place. Over centuries a causeway was built, crowned in 1901 with a standard gauge light railway from Pontorson; this closed in 1938 in the face of motor traffic which spread its parking all along the bank and over the adjacent beach (except at highest tides!) in burgeoning hideous volume. An evil side-effect of the causeway had been ever-worse silting, impairing the tides round le Mont. In recent years authority at last stepped in with plans to replace the causeway with long low viaduct to be served only by park-and-ride buses, the P to be at La Caserne, last shore stop, and R a handful of minibuses for Mont residents and handicapés, the rare Citaros from Pontorson, a couple of horse-drawn charbancs and, titled Le Passeur, six Portuguese Cobus-Contrac purpose-designed double-ended buses!

At the time of our visit this scheme was not completed and these buses terminated on a rather curtailed causeway with a walk onwards through temporary spoil banks of dug-away embankment. Furthermore, short of La Caserne we hit a traffic jam caused, I reckoned, by various motorists arguing the toss rather than accepting P&R. Better control appears necessary. Time will tell!

Once on le Mont the Grande Rue was naturally horribly full of... well, shall I call them pilgrims? At a café with a terrace giving onto the ramparts, we drank essential beer, thence passed onto the ramparts, much more peaceful and less crowded, and climbed many steps, until we realised we were on that section of rampart portrayed in our etching, (reason, be it remembered, why we were here). So we returned down and headed along the tranquil sands until we reached the very spot where Axel Haig must have set up his easel for the original; for both Robin and me, a moment of almost unbelievable triumph.

From ramparts or beach, we could see a perpetual considerable queue for P&R, so I decided that, though it was more than an hour until the time of our bus back to Pontorson, we should return at least as far as la Caserne forthwith, as the queue might not let us onto the last bus to Pontorson when we wished, whereas matters at la Caserne, where we wanted to tarry anyway, would be safer. When the queue let us we boarded one of these extraordinary double-ended buses. In pictures they appear to have half cabs with open platforms, and while they indeed have half cabs the platforms are merely an extra cowl round a motor at either end; what a disappointment! Inside, apart from doors – necessarily – on both sides, is just like any common bus.

We caught the bus before the last bus back to Pontorson, brief sections of former tramway formation noted here and there, and the windmill of Moidrey with sails turning. With time to spare we repaired to the high street, formerly the main road but now bypassed and so mercifully peaceful, and very pleasant to take beer on a terrace in these soporific surroundings on a sunny afternoon. In due time back to la gare, where we admired a handsome but ruinous late C19th mansion, and its concrete water tower, apparently a pioneer in the art. The house and presumably the water tower were temptingly for sale, but probably at vast expense and requiring huge sums spending on them thereafter, and, pleasant though Pontorson be, one might not want to end one's days there.

While waiting for our St. Malo bus we saw the only really decent bus I spotted in the whole three days,

Keolis also runs Mercedes-Benz Citaros in St. Malo. Note the deep glazing in the centre of the bus.

a great long three-axle affair reminding me of those I have loved in Luxembourg, but it was not our bus and did not tarry so I can tell but little of it.

Soon afterwards our bus materialised, the summer-only service operated by Illenoo. As the route serves several well-populated villages I hope it has some sort of service the rest of the year. The bus headed onto the D797, and flanks of hills closed in to our left, once the coast but now with polders on former flat sea-bed on the right. There were a dozen or

13 windmills on the next dozen or 13 kilometres after we struck the coast at Cherrieux, but only the first had sails, not turning, and they were all just variations on the usual drum tower. I know of no other bus route so copiously windmill-decorated. The bus kept up a good pace, and I cannot recall many – if any – local passengers boarding or alighting

Beyond St Benoît-des-Ondes, we left the shore (and accompanying fishy – literally – tourist traps) and soon encountered the bus shelter of la Ville ès Gris, and Cancale, and thus onwards to St. Malo on the route of a couple of days ago, then a 1 or 2 or 3 back to the Porte St. Vincent.

The following morning we trudged to Bretagne, and last step on French soil…

Of course I hope we may soon return - not wait another five years - and meanwhile I can look daily at the etching of the Mont St. Michel.

Yes, I have proved to Robin that it is a real place! ∎

LEFT: **The double-ended Portugese-built shuttle buses have four doors, two on each side.**

BELOW: **A shuttle bus with Mont St. Michel in the background.**

Crosville Cymru

John Young illustrates a selection of the vehicles operated by Crosville Wales.

C rosville Wales came in to being in August 1986, following the split of National Bus Company subsidiary Crosville Motor Services in to two parts. It was bought by its management in December 1987, passing to National Express in January 1989 and then to Drawlane in July 1991. Drawlane became British Bus and then Arriva. Arriva Cymru was formed in April 1998. ∎

ABOVE: **Rhyl, August 1986**
Thirty ex-Southdown Daimler Fleetlines came in to the Crosville fleet to expand double-deck operation, with bodywork split equally between Northern Counties and ECW. Six of the former became open-toppers, named after Welsh castles – in this case, Harlech.

BELOW: **Frongoch Lead Mines, September 1986**
A long Series-A model Leyland National operates a morning journey on the lengthy and scenic Pontrhydfendigaid circular from Aberystwyth, which spent most of its time on narrow country lanes, serving isolated communities. Eight different service numbers (S62-S69) were needed to cover all the various daily route deviations.

Colwyn Bay, June 1987
A large number of dual-purpose Leyland Nationals were inherited by Crosville Wales and carried this bright green and white livery, a marked improvement over NBC green.

Carmel Moors, January 1987
A brief period of competition on traditional Silver Star routes occurred in the early days of deregulation. One of six Bristol LHs to transfer to the new Crosville Wales company is seen thus deployed.

ABOVE: Queensferry, January 1994
The last batch of double-deckers purchased by the Crosville company were dual-purpose Leyland Olympians for the prestigious Cymru Coastliner service, providing a fast hourly service along the coast. They were delivered in 1985.

TOP RIGHT: Penygwryd, June 1994
Four B-series Leyland Nationals transferred from London & Country entered service in L&C livery. They were regulars on the Snowdon Sherpa services but only lasted in the fleet for a maximum of three and a half years. Many of the second-hand acquisitions of the period were similarly short-lived.

BOTTOM RIGHT: Pandy Tudur, January 1995
New investment often came in the form of minibuses. This Marshall-bodied Mercedes-Benz 709D was four months old when photographed on a Llanrwst local service.

TOP LEFT:
Ynyslas Turn,
May 1998
A pair of Leyland Swifts new to Luton and District joined the fleet, working in the South Cambrian division. After four years service they left for Guernsey. They had Wadham Stringer Vanguard bodies.

MIDDLE LEFT:
Llanddulas,
July 1998
Many Bristol VRTs served the company, both new and second-hand from various sources. This home-grown example was new in 1980.

BOTTOM LEFT:
Llandudno,
July 1998
Numerically the last double decker to be purchased by the Crosville company, dual-purpose ECW-bodied Leyland Olympian EOG212 (C212 GTU) was later converted to open-top and is now preserved.

TOP RIGHT:
Penmaenmawr,
November 1998
Leyland Lynxes became the pre-owned single-decker of choice, with examples new to the fleets of Colchester, Atlas Bus, Moordale and Chesterfield Transport acquired, along with an ex-demonstrator from McGill's and former Halton examples acquired through the Devaway business. Under Arriva control, West Riding was added to the list. This bus was new to Chesterfield.

BOTTOM RIGHT:
Dyserth,
June 2001
Under Arriva stewardship, increased investment came in the form of a significant number of Mini Pointer Darts, ideal for many of the routes previously run by minibuses. No Dennis Darts carried Crosville Wales colours as the only two Darts purchased pre-Arriva carried a promotional livery highlighting their low-floor credentials. Dyserth is served by a circular route linking it to Rhyl and Prestatyn.

Deregulated Portsmouth
- the first five years

Between Deregulation on 26 October 1986 and the replacement of Portsmouth Transit's full-size buses with minibuses by August 1991, Portsmouth's bus users had a choice of 16 operators. **David Jukes** unravels the story.

All photographs by the author.

BACKGROUND

The 1985 Transport Act brought an end to the Portsmouth Area Joint Transport Services Agreement between the City of Portsmouth Passenger Transport Department (CPPTD) and Southdown Motor Services. This had started on 1 July 1946 and had been revised in 1967.

CPPTD was the city's municipal operator, starting as Portsmouth Corporation Tramways on 1 January 1901 and receiving its revised title on 16 June 1936. Its final livery was white with crimson skirt panels.

Southdown had been incorporated on 2 June 1915 and its ownership transferred from Tilling & British Automobile Traction to the British Electric Traction group in 1942. The latter was sold to the Transport Holding Company in 1968 and Southdown became part of the resultant National Bus Company; from 1973 its buses were painted in NBC leaf green livery, and its coaches white.

In preparation for NBC privatisation, a new logo was introduced featuring a lazy S shape on a green background to represent a rolling road across the hills of the South Downs (and quickly dubbed Hissing Sid by many), and the company's traditional apple green and cream colours returned.

PORTSMOUTH CITY TRANSPORT

On 26 October 1986 CPPTD's assets were taken over

Illustrating how things used to be, the oldest ex-Portsmouth Atlantean owned by Portsmouth Transit was 1973-built 287 (XTP 287L), which was repainted in full City of Portsmouth livery by Transit Holdings. It was retained by Blue Admiral until transfer to Thames Transit in 1996.

by council-owned Portsmouth City Transport Ltd, with CPPTD's final general manager, Eric Boyes, as its managing director. The inherited fleet consisted of 93 Leyland Atlantean AN68s, seven Leyland National 2s, three Dennis Lancet midibuses and a second-hand Leyland Leopard coach. There were also six open-top Leylands – one Titan and five PDR1/1 Atlanteans.

Vehicle liveries were initially unchanged but the city crest was replaced by a new logo based on the outline of Portsea Island and its surrounding coastline. Livery experiments saw two Atlanteans, receive dark blue skirts and engine covers while another two had these same areas painted sky blue and signal red respectively. Ermine and signal red were adopted as the new PCT livery, applied in the same layout latterly used by CPPTD.

The coach fleet was expanded in 1987 with the acquisition of two 1973 Leyland Leopards from Bournemouth and the conversion of a dual-door Atlantean to single-door form with high-backed seating.

Most weekday daytime services were registered commercially and PCT successfully bid for unregistered early morning and late evening Monday to Saturday services put out to tender by Hampshire County Council (HCC). PCT deliberately chose not to run Sunday bus services because of staff problems; these were instead operated by Southdown which successfully bid for the HCC tender.

PCT extended its services beyond the city boundary to compete with Southdown on the Waterlooville and Wecock Farm routes, but was forced by staff shortages to de-register a Cosham local service and evening journeys on Paulsgrove area routes; these were put out to tender and won by the Provincial Bus Company.

Eric Boyes considered there was sufficient potential in PCT to propose a management buy-out during 1987. This was declined by the city council and Boyes left for Scarborough & District at the end of that year.

However commercial pressures brought about by the forthcoming introduction of a minibus operation to be run jointly by Badgerline and Southampton City Transport led the city council to put PCT on the market in November 1987. The highest bid was received from Southern Vectis but bidding was re-opened to allow PCT's employees a second chance to mount a successful bid. Southern Vectis again triumphed but negotiations bogged down amid the city council's refusal to dispose of its property, and its insistence on minimum service levels. Threatened redundancies and route franchising were also unacceptable to the council.

The PCT employees then approached Southampton City Transport to join their bid, and the Start Right

The UOR-T batch of 1978/79 Alexander AL-bodied Leyland Atlantean AN68A/1Rs were among the first to receive the Portsmouth City Transport ermine white and signal red bus livery. 333 (UOR 333T) is accompanied by one of the 1972-built VTP-L registered batch of similar buses based on the AN68/1R chassis and still in white and crimson.

1979 Alexander-bodied Leyland Atlantean 340 (YBK 340V) received this eye-catching ice-blue livery at the same time as dark blue was tried on two others. It is seen outside Portsmouth & Southsea railway station on route to Leigh Park.

In newly-applied Portsmouth Citybus livery, complete with the Citybus fleetnames which replaced earlier Portsmouth Citybus labels, is 316 (HOR 316N), a 1975 Alexander-bodied Leyland Atlantean in Commercial Road in May 1989.

Cooperative Ltd took over on 10 June 1988 with 75 per cent owned by SCT (then still wholly-owned by Southampton City Council) and the remaining 25 per cent by 147 PCT employees.

SOUTHDOWN

The other pre-deregulation incumbent, Southdown Motor Services, with Philip Ayers as general manager, had its headquarters at Lewes, East Sussex. Vehicle exchanges between NBC subsidiaries were commonplace in the run up to deregulation and in October 1986 Southdown acquired 19 Leyland Nationals and four Bristol VRTs from Ribble.

These were allocated to the company's Hampshire division and added a further livery variation to the city as all bar one of the VRTs entered service in NBC poppy red (the exception carried a National Travelworld overall advertisement). A further six VRTs were acquired from Devon General, five of which entered service in poppy red (the other in leaf green) although two were quickly repainted into a blue livery for the Havant Hypermarket free bus services. All were repainted green and cream in due course.

As previously stated, Southdown operated Portsmouth's Sunday bus services after successfully bidding for the work. It later took on more evening journeys and other work within the city as PCT struggled on. Southdown became independent of NBC from 2 October 1987 after a management-led buyout.

Few buses were subsequently acquired as Southdown's operating area shrunk along its north-eastern boundaries, but these did include the only new buses to be bought by the independent Southdown – 12 Northern Counties-bodied Volvo B10M Citybuses in August 1989.

Southdown 660 (AAP 660T), a 1978 ECW-bodied Bristol VRT, was one of a number in the fleet converted from dual to single-door form – the centre staircase remaining in place. It illustrates the revival of Southdown's traditional green to replace the darker shade used by NBC.

Five of the six ex-Grampian Atlanteans acquired by Stagecoach Portsmouth were repainted into full-corporate livery with Portsmouth fleetnames. 319 (KSA 189P) loads in Edinburgh Road in April 1990.

Almost simultaneously, Southdown was sold to the Stagecoach group, on 16 August, and Brian Souter was appointed interim managing director until the permanent appointment of Brian Cox at the start of October.

RED ADMIRAL

But we now need to step back to October 1987 and take a look at the joint Badgerline/Southampton City Transport minibus operation proposed for Portsmouth. This materialised in the form of Quayshelfco 179 Ltd, trading as Red Admiral, registered for the operation of 46 vehicles. Its registered office was Badgerline's headquarters in Weston-super-Mare, with operating centres at Quartremaine Road, Portsmouth, and at SCT's Portswood base in Southampton.

Red Admiral's first service, the A1 between Portsea and Paulsgrove, started on 11 December 1987 using 15 red and black-liveried Robin Hood-bodied Iveco minibuses licensed to Badgerline. Further services were introduced on 21 March and 13 May 1988 – the new company now serving Eastney and Waterlooville in competition with Portsmouth City Transport and Southdown.

By April 1988 the licence holder was Pathfinder UK Ltd with the equity divided between Badgerline (47.5 per cent), SCT (47.5 per cent) and general manager Alan Barrett (5 per cent). The extended network required additional vehicles for which 15 similar Ivecos were acquired (seating 23 instead of 19), still licensed by Badgerline but this time paid for and registered by SCT.

After Portsmouth City Transport came under Southampton City Transport control in June 1988, SCT then acquired Badgerline's share in Pathfinder UK in July.

PORTSMOUTH CITYBUS

The former municipal operation acquired by Start Right Cooperative had become Portsmouth Citybus Ltd on 25 July 1988. The fleet remained almost unchanged from

Numerically the last Leyland Atlantean in the Portsmouth municipal fleet, 354 (CPO 354W) is seen in Southdown Portsmouth ownership in July 1990 heading through Portsmouth city centre to Wecock Farm. Nine of the batch of ten which were bodied by East Lancs passed to the Sheffield Omnibus Company after withdrawal by Portsmouth Transit the following year – the exception was a fire victim.

that inherited by PCT from CPPTD in October 1986 – the two ex-Bournemouth Leopard coaches had been added and three Alexander-bodied Atlanteans withdrawn in the meantime.

Portsmouth Citybus and plain Citybus fleetnames were applied; the latter on repaints into the Southampton red and cream livery adopted by the new company. Coaches and the open-top fleet were earmarked to receive the all-over Red Ensign livery and branding – the Titan and three Atlanteans missed out and retained PCT colours.

Portsmouth Citybus started to update its fleet in mid-1989. Out went some of the older Atlantean AN68s and in came 12 second-hand Leyland Nationals from London Buses – ten for service and a pair for spares. These were almost identical in specification to the 14 bought new by CPPTD in 1976 and sold just five years later...

By this time the Pathfinder UK office had moved to that of Portsmouth Citybus at Eastney, with former Pathfinder UK manager Alan Barrett now managing both. Barrett sold his Pathfinder UK shares to Southampton City Transport and Pathfinder UK ceased trading on 2 October 1989. The SCT-owned Red Admiral Ivecos were added to the Portsmouth Citybus fleet while the Badgerline-owned batch were returned off-lease, although eight were briefly loaned to Portsmouth Citybus.

PEOPLE'S PROVINCIAL

There was another main player in the Portsmouth bus market by this time. Employee-owned Provincial Bus

Stagecoach Southdown soon realised investment in new buses for its Portsmouth operations was required and eight of its first batch of ten standard Alexander RL-bodied Leyland Olympians were allocated to Eastney from new. An immaculate and very new 702 (G702 TCD) loads in Portsmouth city centre in April 1990.

The five former Grampian Leyland Atlanteans painted into corporate livery by Stagecoach Portsmouth received this modified scheme in subsequent Portsmouth Transit ownership – the orange band was simply painted out. 316 (KSA 182P) exits Commercial Road in May 1991.

ABOVE LEFT: **This ex-Southdown Leyland National in Portsmouth Transit ownership, CBV 777S, retained Southdown livery but with new fleetnames when it was photographed at South Parade Pier, Southsea, in January 1991. Note the advert for Southdown Motor Service's Green Card. This was one of a number of Nationals acquired by Yorkshire Terrier after they were replaced by minibuses.**

ABOVE RIGHT: **Stagecoach retained its Havant road routes 21 and 23 on divesting the majority of its Portsmouth-based operations. Carrying Stagecoach stripes and Southdown identity in corporate style in August 1991 are this pair of ECW-bodied Bristol VRTs – 1981-built 268 (JWV 268W) leading 1979-built 677 (EAP 977V) south from Commercial Road.**

Company, trading as People's Provincial after its buy-out from NBC in May 1987, painted its buses emerald green and cream to reflect the history of the pre-NBC Provincial business. Red-painted wheels were an eye-catching addition.

The company moved into Portsmouth in August 1987, successfully bidding for the Cosham night bus network after Portsmouth City Transport withdrew the evening journeys on its four Paulsgrove routes. To these was added the Highbury to Wymering local route after another Hampshire County Council tender win.

People's Provincial chose not to bid for Portsmouth City Transport despite three invitations by Portsmouth City Council to do so. It instead chose to increase the

company's presence within Portsmouth and started its own commercial services on 10 June 1988 – the 48/49 Paulsgrove to Fareham via Portsea Island circulars and the Fareham to Southsea route 50.

Nineteen Leyland Nationals had been acquired from National Welsh the previous November, to which were added six former Southdown Nationals from Ensignbus and three more of the type from Rennie's of Dunfermline – most were allocated to the Portsmouth operation.

Other routes subsequently introduced included the Sunrider route 70 open-top service using an ex-Southdown Titan PD3/4 and a weekday route 66 connecting Portsmouth's tourist attractions – also open-topped.

STAGECOACH EXPANSION – AND CONTRACTION

A further change in Portsmouth's bus operators occurred on 20 October 1989 with Stagecoach's acquisition of Southampton's 75 per cent stake in Portsmouth Citybus (the employees sold their share the following week) just two months after buying Southdown. Southampton Citybus maintained a presence in Portsmouth as it took over the 727 express

BELOW LEFT: **The final batch of second-hand Leyland Nationals acquired by People's Provincial included 403 (AYR 299T), see here in Edinburgh Road in July 1991. It had been new to London Transport in 1979.**

BELOW RIGHT: **Laying over in Portsmouth Road, Cosham, is GTP 166F, a 1967 Metro-Cammell-bodied Leyland Panther Cub which had been new to Portsmouth. It was owned by Cosham Coaches between February 1985 and March 1990. Note the comprehensive destination display for the operator's route 101.**

Carrying the smart red, white and blue Hampshire Bus livery at the South Parade Pier terminus is the operator's 2410 (BFX 578T), a 1979 ECW-bodied Bristol VRT which had been new to Hants & Dorset.

service between the two cities as part of the deal. It had shared the route with Southdown after Hampshire Bus pulled out of Southampton. (Hampshire Bus itself worked into Portsmouth from October 1986 after extending its Winchester to Fareham route 69 on to Southsea).

Southampton Citybus retained ownership of the three Portsmouth Citybus coaches, the trio of Lancet midibuses and an open-top Atlantean. Fleet reinforcements arrived in the shape of six 1975 Alexander-bodied Atlanteans from Stagecoach East Midlands' defunct Frontrunner North West subsidiary. These had been new to Grampian Regional Transport. The buses entered service in the green and cream livery in which they were received.

The Portsmouth business briefly traded as Stagecoach Portsmouth, with an Atlantean, 333, being the first to receive Stagecoach stripes. It was absorbed by Southdown on 1 January 1990 and a new Southdown Portsmouth trading name adopted for the area's Stagecoach operations, now based at the leased ex-CPPTD Eastney depot. Southdown's Hilsea depot was used as a vehicle store.

Service and timetable rationalisation meant the six acquired Atlanteans and existing Southdown stock could effectively replace 48 early ex-CPPTD Atlantean AN68s which were not operated by their new owner because they lacked power steering. Four of the open-top buses (the Titan and three Atlanteans) were placed in store and not operated either.

The Department of Trade & Industry referred Stagecoach's purchase of Portsmouth Citybus to the Monopolies & Mergers Commission on 21 February 1990. A report published in July concluded Stagecoach's dominance could deter competitors but public interest was not adversely affected. It did not recommend the sale be undone because of the subsequent rationalisation of operations, but set in place safeguards relating to reducing fares and increasing headways against any competitor.

All this was acceptable to Stagecoach, but not to Nicholas Ridley, the secretary of state for trade and industry. He directed Stagecoach to divest itself of Portsmouth Citybus. Southdown Portsmouth reorganised – Leigh Park, Havant and Hayling remained in Stagecoach ownership with the Eastney operations to be divested. Reallocations moved the better vehicles out; their places taken by ageing Hastings & District stock working alongside former Portsmouth and Grampian Atlanteans and ex-Ribble Nationals earmarked for disposal.

TRANSIT HOLDINGS

The reason for the stock changes became clear with the sale by Stagecoach of Southdown's Portsmouth division to Transit Holdings on 19 January 1991. Experience elsewhere indicated that minibuses would soon replace the acquired 100-strong fleet. The latter carried a comprehensive livery mix with combined Portsmouth Transit, Red Admiral, Blue Admiral fleetnames covering

This former London Transport AEC single-deck bus in the White Heather fleet was EGN 441J, a Park Royal-bodied Swift which had latterly been used by LT as a recruitment vehicle. Reverting to bus use, the Swift is seen in Commercial Road in June 1989.

those applied by previous operators. The Stagecoach livery on a number of buses was amended – orange stripes were painted out on some, and another received three red stripes.

But most simply carried on until replacement by Ford Transit and Mercedes-Benz minibuses operating in Blue Admiral colours on city services, and Red Admiral livery for the out-of-city routes. The Blue Admirals were based at the reopened Hilsea West garage and the Red Admirals at Harts Farm, Havant. Transit Holdings retained 1972 Atlantean 287 – now resplendent in CPPTD livery – and later acquired the former CPPTD Titan open-topper from Stagecoach in a separate deal.

Stagecoach retained its Havant Road services. The majority of vehicles in Stagecoach stripes initially ran with the Portsmouth part of their Southdown Portsmouth fleetnames blanked out until these were replaced with corporate-style Southdown fleetnames once again. Others retained Southdown green and cream.

People's Provincial expanded as Transit Holdings converted to minibus operation, actively marketing itself as the big bus alternative. Two new services from Paulsgrove were started and its existing routes revised before introducing competing routes from Waterlooville to Portsmouth and Fareham on 18 February 1991.

More direct competition started on 3 June with the introduction of routes 27 and 28 which shadowed Blue Admiral's routes 17 and 18. People's Provincial soon renumbered their services as the 17 and 18 which led to a Blue Admiral court injunction and a further renumbering to 117 and 118.

People's Provincial required additional buses to meet its new obligations and 14 Leyland Nationals were acquired from London Buses, the last of the type purchased by the operator. Also acquired at this time were a pair of convertible open-top Daimler Fleetlines from Yellow Buses, Bournemouth, for the Sunrider 70 service during summer months.

THE SMALLER OPERATORS

Amidst this jockeying for position by the big operators, Portsmouth was also served by a handful of smaller businesses. Cosham Coaches operated route 101 between Horndean and Portsmouth via the city's hospitals from 27 October 1986. Four return journeys were worked Mondays to Fridays (three on Saturdays) using one of three ex-Portsmouth buses then owned, a 1967 Panther Cub and two 1969 AEC Swifts.

A route 102 was simultaneously operated between The Hard Interchange and Southsea via the city centre until October 1988 when it was replaced by a new route 102 which linked Hambledon and Southsea. This was usually operated by a former Yellow Buses Bournemouth Atlantean which retained its former owner's livery in its entirety until the service ceased in December 1988.

White Heather Travel route 45 linked Hambledon and Waterlooville as a county council tendered service,

People's Provincial Leyland National 413 (AYR 341T) entered service in London Buses colours. The bus was new in 1979 and is seen in Paulsgrove, in August 1991 three months after arriving from the capital.

TOP LEFT: **The Leyland Panther Cub was always a rare beast; this example particularly so as it was still in frontline service when photographed in Portsmouth city centre in May 1991 by which time it was 24 years old. Metro-Cammell-bodied GTP 175F was new to Portsmouth in 1967. After being bought for preservation it joined the Solent Beeline fleet in 1989, where it ran for two years. The bus now forms part of the City of Portsmouth Preserved Transport Depot collection and is stored pending full restoration.**

MIDDLE LEFT: **Adding its distinctive colours to Portsmouth is former Solent Blue Line JTH 756P, a 1975 Leyland National new to South Wales Transport, which operated on hire to Priory Coaches before being purchased and repainted white. It is seen in Portsmouth city centre in May 1991.**

BOTTOM LEFT: **The latter years of Hants & Sussex saw a number of former London Transport and London Country AEC Merlins and Swifts in regular use. AML 567H, seen here in Edinburgh Road in May 1991, first entered service with LT in 1970 on Red Arrow services. It was acquired by Hants & Sussex in 1989.**

but certain journeys were extended into Portsmouth. The latter operated on weekdays only from October 1988 until the company's licence was surrendered on 17 November 1989, a week before it was due to face a Department of Transport inquiry over alleged improper running. Vehicles used included a former London Transport AEC Merlin and AEC Swift.

Hants & Sussex was the revived name for Basil Williams' operations in Hampshire and West Sussex. A West Sussex County Council-tendered Saturday-only route 22 was operated as one return journey from Petworth to Portsmouth, replacing a Southdown route from June 1989.

This was followed in November 1989 by a Hampshire council contract to run the ex-White Heather route 45. This was usually operated by former London Transport AEC Merlins and Swifts until the contract's expiry in June 1990 when it was awarded to Southdown. Hants & Sussex continued to commercially work some route 45 journeys in competition; these were renumbered 451 in July 1990 with some of the fleet's Leyland Leopards sharing duties with the ex-London stock.

Solent Beeline operated route 100 on a daily basis between The Hard Interchange and the Continental Ferry Port via the city centre from 1 February 1990.

The main vehicle used was a 1967 ex-Portsmouth Leyland Panther Cub until its replacement by a former Grampian Atlantean brought to Portsmouth by Stagecoach.

Priory Coaches operated route 80 between The Hard Interchange and the city centre during 1991 using second-hand Leyland Nationals painted white with brown trim.

Adding further colour to the Portsmouth roads each summer were Guide Friday's open-top city tour buses, which first appeared in summer 1990. Buses were taken from the unallocated pool and carried generic tour legends on the operator's dark green and cream livery – a mix of Leyland Atlanteans, Daimler Fleetlines and Bristol VRTs were the usual fare.

POSTSCRIPT

Much happened to Portsmouth's bus services during the five post-deregulation years, not all of it necessarily benefiting the fare-paying passengers.

Nowadays, Stagecoach South retains its Portsmouth to Havant services while the Red Admiral, Blue Admiral and People's Provincial operations are part of First Hampshire & Dorset. The Southampton express service 727 has been replaced by First's X4 route after different operators attempted to make a success of it, while Hampshire Bus route 69 terminates at Fareham once again. The other operators have all since ceased trading.

With grateful thanks to Robert Smith for his assistance in clarifying matters. ∎

Ailsa Oddities

The Ailsa is a model inextricably linked with the Scottish Bus Group but, as **Billy Nicol** illustrates, many small Scottish operators bought second-hand Ailsas.

ABOVE: **A1 Service of Ardrossan bought Ailsas new and secondhand. With its Alexander body this bus is broadly similar to some of those bought new by A1, but it is in fact a former Maidstone & District bus, one of five bought by M&D for evaluation.**

TOP LEFT: **M-Line of Alloa operated this Northern Counties-bodied Ailsa, which was one of three bought by the Greater Manchester PTE. It is seen in Glasgow on a football supporters' hire in 1994.**

BOTTOM LEFT: **Among the large fleet of conventional rear-engined double-deckers operated by Rennie of Dunfermline in the 1990s were three Alexander-bodied Ailsas which had been new to Western SMT.**

TOP RIGHT: A number of the Alexander-bodied Ailsas which had been new to the West Midlands PTE reached Scotland after a short spell operating for London Buses. Still in London livery, this bus was owned by Silver Fox of Renfrew.

MIDDLE RIGHT: Well known as an operator of luxury coaches, Doig's of Glasgow also ran double-deck buses. One was the unique low-height Ailsa with Alexander body which had been new to Derby. It is seen with Doig's in 1998 and is now preserved.

BELOW: Marbill of Beith operated a number of Ailsas on contract and private hire work. This example came from Kelvin Central but had been new in 1977 to Alexander Midland.

ABOVE: **Over the years Irvine of Law, in Lanarkshire, has operated many types of double-decker including this former Tayside Northern Counties-bodied Ailsa seen in 2002. Irvine ceased operations in 2012.**

TOP RIGHT: **A pair of Alexander-bodied Ailsas in the fleet of Clyde Coast, Ardrossan in 2002. The bus on the left, a Mark III with raised driving position, originated with Tayside; that on the right was new to the neighbouring A1 business.**

BOTTOM RIGHT: **Former Tayside Ailsas proved popular with Scottish independents. This Northern Counties-bodied bus is seen in Glasgow with McDade's of Uddingston.**

The **WOW** factor

Peter Rowlands picks out developments in bus design and presentation that have fired his enthusiasm over the decades, and despite setbacks have kept him looking to the future.

All photographs by the author.

FRONT TO BACK

Try to imagine a world where more or less all double-decker buses had their engine at the front and an open platform at the back. That sums up in Newcastle upon Tyne in the late 1950s.

Suddenly, the Leyland Atlantean. The extraordinary impact of this bus is hard now to convey. So much of the Atlantean was different. It wasn't just that the positions of the engine and the doorway had been switched, it was the implications of all this: the flat front; the low driving position and unobstructed forward view; the folding platform doors (more or less unknown in my area); the forward staircase. Then there was that clutchless Pneumocyclic gearbox with its diminutive gear lever sprouting from the steering column.

The Atlantean put Leyland at the forefront of bus design. Almost exactly 30 years later, in 1988, its bus business was bought by Volvo and disappeared as a brand; but the principles of the Atlantean have become almost universal, so its legacy lives on.

Dating from 1963, this Atlantean with Metro-Cammell bodywork is similar to Newcastle's earliest examples, except that it has twin headlamps instead of the singles of the original deliveries. It is seen in a short-lived mainly-cream Tyne & Wear PTE livery in Blackett Street in the city in 1976.

SINGLE-DECKERS REBORN

In my memory, most of the single-decker buses of my childhood were relatively short, high-floor vehicles – the Leyland Tiger Cub, the Bristol LS and MW. I had nothing against them, but they didn't set my world alight either. Then one day I was sitting on the top deck of a Newcastle double-decker, passing the thronging Haymarket bus station, when I saw my first Bristol RE in the livery of United Auto.

Bearing the later deep-screen version of ECW's flat-fronted bodywork, this Bristol RE of United Counties dates from 1969. Still in service in 1986, it had by then acquired Hitchin Bus fleetnames and a somewhat multi-coloured livery.

It was astounding. Not only was it nicely styled, with its low-slung body and contoured front end, but it also seemed long: extremely long. I could hardly believe such a vehicle could be permitted, or would be capable of negotiating the bends of a typical bus route.

Other models of single-decker bus in that period were also long and low, of course – the Leyland Panther, for instance, and the AEC Swift. And in the 1980s, political shenanigans brought an end to RE production in favour of the Leyland National. But for me none of these ever achieved the definitive look or impact of the Bristol RE.

STILL IN THE GAME

I was standing under a flyover hitch-hiking with a friend when I saw my first Bristol VR double-decker in 1968, probably on delivery to its operator. "Look – a Bristol Atlantean!" he exclaimed, showing admirable grasp of the notion of a new rear-engined double-decker, if not of the subtleties of branding.

To me, it was a revelation. It meant that Bristol, up till then only producing front-engined double-deckers, planned to stay in the game, competing with Leyland's Atlantean and Daimler's Fleetline. And so it proved; the VR continued in production until 1981, becoming one of the stalwarts of the British bus building industry.

The initial 1960s ECW body design for the Bristol VRT featured a flat lower front end with divided windscreen. This Ribble example dating from 1970 has since been celebrated as an EFE model in its original maroon livery. It is seen in Carlisle in 1978.

1970s

LEYLAND CHALLENGER

By the 1970s, virtually all double-deck bus manufacture in Britain was controlled by British Leyland, but that wouldn't last, and the first real taste of a complete double-decker from a company outside Leyland's empire was MCW's Metropolitan, created with the help of running units from Scania.

The Metropolitan was amazingly quiet, and its air suspension offered a soft if slightly wallowing ride. Also it looked remarkable. Arguably it was one of the first modern double-deckers conceived and styled as a complete, coherent entity: square and boxy, yes, but not relentlessly square. The designers understood the need for rounded edges. They also repeated the distinctive asymmetric windscreen that they'd used on their Metro-Scania single-decker. And wonder of wonders, the back was flush: no hint of the engine pod that muddled the back end of most other rear-engined double-deck designs.

The Metropolitan may have suffered engineering and corrosion problems later on, but visually it set a standard that was hard to beat.

The MCW Metropolitan was one of the first double-decker buses that could claim a fully integrated design, visually as well as in engineering terms. Greater Glasgow acquired 40 in 1974, and this one is seen three years later.

LANCASHIRE LOOK

I can't really claim to have been inspired by the wonderful Mancunian double-decker; I'm sure I would have been, but it was already out of production by the time I first saw one. Instead, new deliveries in Manchester from then on were the neat but much less dramatic Standards from Northern Counties and other builders, which set the pattern for double-deckers countrywide for many years to come.

I liked those well enough, but it was the East Lancashire Coachbuilders body of that period that somehow appealed to me more. In a way it was the company's take on the Standard look, but its crisp, square styling and slightly peaked front dome seemed to me to have more flair; they said bus design was still moving forward.

This body design became the de facto standard for early Dominators – the model that marked Dennis's return to the bus market. East Lancs is no longer with us, of course – swallowed up by Optare – but as part of ADL, Dennis still is.

The crisp styling of East Lancashire Coachbuilders' standard 1970s body worked well on the Dennis Dominator. Leicester City Transport was an enthusiastic customer, and acquired this example in 1977. It was photographed in March 1982.

1980s

FAILED POTENTIAL

Double-deck coaches were by no means unknown in the 1980s, but they almost all came from continental manufacturers. Then in 1983 MCW amazed the market with the launch of its UK-built Metroliner range. Admittedly, the high-roof double-deck design drew on the company's existing Metrobus, and the overall look bore more than a passing resemblance to the Van Hool coach range of the day. Never mind; it was stylish and dramatic, and seemed to say MCW was here for the long haul.

Sadly, that promise was never fulfilled. They were too tall for the continental market, and the support system from MCW didn't convince independent coach operators, who saw the Metroliner as basically an overblown bus. National Bus Company took more than a hundred, and a few others went to operators in public ownership, but that was that. Within six years, MCW itself had ceased trading.

Still, in the day those three-axle coaches looked stately and convincing, and many lived on as sightseeing buses for years afterwards.

MCW's Metroliner double-deck coach design looked impressive in this livery used by London Buses, which acquired four examples in the mid-1980s. This one is seen at Victoria on the London to Birmingham service in June 1986.

OUT WITH THE CURVES

Walter Alexander, one of Britain's biggest bus bodybuilders, had retained a resolutely rounded look for its bodywork since the 1950s. In the 1960s and 70s, operators who wanted something with more definition were simply offered peaks on the front and (sometimes) rear domes.

However, in 1981 it rung the changes emphatically with its R-type body, which established new styling that endured for a generation. It was neat, contained and unfussy, and seemed much more in keeping with an era in which customer appeal was becoming increasingly important. It became a kind of standard in its own right, and was even copied slavishly by the likes of East Lancashire Coachbuilders in a bid to keep customers happy.

Photographed in Basingstoke in 1988, and evoking a brief period when Stagecoach had launched its stripes but not rolled out its standard logo, this Leyland Olympian of Hampshire Bus carries by-then familiar Alexander R-type bodywork.

1990s

PRESIDENTIAL PRESENCE

The early 1990s gave birth to Northern Counties' Palatine 2 bodywork. The deep, multiple-curvature windscreen of this design, harking back to the Mancunian of twenty years before, gave it a dramatic frontal appearance, and was well matched to the curved upper front windows. Arguably few double-deck designs had been endowed with such stylistic integrity since the Metropolitan.

It was the company's last high-floor double-deck design, and arguably should have stayed in production longer. However, it was replaced within five years by the same company's President body, a design prompted by the industry's rapid switch to low-floor double-deckers towards the end of the decade.

Some features were carried over from the Palatine 2, including the President's striking deep windscreen, but the front upper and lower deck styling failed to offer the same coherent look.

Seen in Liverpool in 1995, this Northern Counties-bodied Volvo Olympian was bought new by Liverbus, a business later acquired by Merseyside Travel. The well-considered body design is summed up by the complementary curved-sided upper and lower front windows.

GOING LOW

It's easy now to overlook the Alexander ALX400 double-decker body, launched in 1997. It's one of the few recent double-deck bodies built in thousands rather than hundreds, and became almost the de facto standard bus around the turn of the century. Eventually it seemed almost boring, and it was a relief when Alexander Dennis launched its replacement, the Enviro400, in 2005.

Yet in the day it represented a major leap forward from the R-type, and a demonstration that the company still had plenty of design flair. It helped launch the low-floor double-decker concept to the UK market, and it's only fitting that the first example, based on a DAF chassis, should already have been preserved.

2000s

THE NOKIA LOOK

For those with long memories, Wrightbus is still the new kid on the block when it comes to double-decker buses. Although an old company, it only launched its first double-deck body, the Eclipse Gemini, in 2001. But what an enduring design it proved. With detailed variations, the underlying Gemini styling has been offered on a variety of chassis and underframes ever since.

The noisiness of the Volvo B7TL variety has been widely and understandably criticised, but that's no fault of Wrightbus. The Gemini was Wright's declaration that it was a serious UK contender in the bus market of the future, and that claim has been amply borne out in practice, with examples appearing across the world. Those clever matched curving upper and lower front screens, earning the

design the sobriquet 'Nokia bus' in some quarters, gave the Gemini a unique look that has never been paralleled.

Wright's Gemini bodywork looked smart in the full regalia of First's early yellow-look London livery. This Volvo was photographed in May 2005.

SECRET ADMIRATION

I don't really want to like the Scania OmniCity, which often seems to get described as the 'Polish Scania'. Perhaps I subscribe reluctantly to the implication that it doesn't support the UK's fragile home-based bodybuilding industry. Yet I do like it. That neat font end is beautifully well balanced, and is nicely matched by the alignment of the side windows. It picks up design cues from previous models such as Alexander's Royale and Optare's Spectra, and shows just how effectively they can be used.

Basically it's a cautious, reassuring bus. It looks modern without being in any way remarkable; in a sense it's ageless. In a different world we might consider this to be what all buses should look like, but other makers seem to have demonstrated pretty conclusively that imaginative design has somewhat more to offer.

I'll just have to indulge my liking in secret.

Smart but safe – the discreetly stylish Scania OmniCity, here in the fleet of London United (but bearing only a Transdev fleetname). This one is seen at Hammersmith in June 2010.

CORPORATE BUT LOCAL

Can you achieve common branding across an entire bus fleet, either within a given area or across the whole country, yet still provide enough local variation to identify buses with their main operating territory, or even with specific routes?

Token fleetnames do little to associate buses visually with their locality, while comprehensive route-branding tends to remove the visual connection between buses in the same fleet. This was beginning to look like a conundrum too tough to crack.

In their latest form, Reading's multi-coloured liveries carry sub-branding to denote each colour scheme: Scarlet, Claret, Yellow, Purple. Among recent deliveries are all-ADL Enviro400s in a variety of colours.

But not for Reading Buses! Somehow, this operator has pulled off the remarkable feat of creating a whole range of liveries that differ strikingly from each other in both colour and detailing, yet still have overriding coherence. And all this within the environs of a single medium-sized town. In their latest form especially, Reading's liveries are highly effective in their own right – stylish, colourful and exuberant. Many a bus operator would probably be glad to have just one of them.

Reading seems to have rewritten the book on corporate identity, and other operators should perhaps take note.

ENVIRO400 PROGRESS

Are you a fan of Alexander Dennis's Enviro400 body? Personally I've never felt entirely comfortable with the curved 'piano-front' top screen, preferring the more upright, confident look used on the Enviro500 for foreign markets. Then came the announcement of the new Enviro400, with news that the piano-front look would be retained. What a disappointment.

However, when the new body was unveiled, it turned out that the rounded look had been toned down, and sculpted side mouldings added extra interest to the frontal appearance.

That'll do nicely. ■

A new-style ADL Enviro400H in the fleet of Abellio, approaching Croydon in March 2015.